THE GOLD OF QUIVIRA

A STORY OF SPANISH CONQUISTADORES ON THE GREAT PLAINS

Anthony J. Barak, Ph.D.

Writers Club Press
San Jose New York Lincoln Shanghai

The Gold of Quivira
A Story of Spanish Conquistadores on the Great Plains

Published by Writers Club Press
an imprint of iUniverse.com, Inc.

For information address:
iUniverse.com, Inc.
620 North 48th Street
Suite 201
Lincoln, NE 68504-3467
www.iuniverse.com

ISBN: 0-595-00620-5

Printed in the United States of America

DEDICATION

This book is dedicated to my daughter Mary A. Barak-Bernhagen.

Epigraph

From out of Mexico these vampires came,

with gold and silver their lofty goals.

But only the desert would mark its claim,

in blood, in lives and Spanish souls.

...The Author

CONTENTS

PREFACE

It seems almost unbelievable that in less than fifty years after Columbus landed in the West Indies, Spanish conquistadores were roaming the plains of The Great American Desert in their incessant search for native gold. The impetus for these plundering efforts was not only to gain personal wealth, but also to win favor with the king for helping to swell the treasury coffers of the Spanish Empire.

To the Spanish conquerors, no place on the American continent was exempt from their greed which is exemplified in their sacking of the wealth and their ravaging of the people of Mexico. Their insatiable appetite for gold, however, did not end there and before 1600 Spanish caravans were crawling over most of what today is the southwestern portion of the United States even touching and affecting the lives of the Wichita and Pawnee Indians of present-day Kansas and Nebraska. Justifiably, most of the Spanish probes into this territory, earlier known as "Quivira," ended either disastrously or as fruitless quests for riches. Many of the leaders of these expeditions were either killed in their gold-seeking endeavors or returned to Mexico disgraced for their failures to produce expected riches for the Crown.

This work, a historical novel, is a combination of fact and fiction and is an attempt at portraying the lifestyle and experiences of the large Pawnee Nation as they fought for survival on the vast grasslands of the Great American Desert. It is the purpose of this writing to demonstrate the problems faced by these people in this raw land that were brought on not only by their traditional enemies, but also by the invasion of the hairy white men, particularly the gold-seeking, ruthless, armored marauders of Spanish Mexico.

Chapter I

The Origin

In very early times, the Pawnee Indians were the largest and most powerful populace on the western plain. These people were derived from the Caddoan linguistic stock whose early home existed in eastern Oklahoma and western Arkansas. In their northern migration to hunt the buffalo, the tribe divided when reaching southern Kansas. The group leaving the main body remained in Kansas and eventually became the Wichita tribe, while the main group continued its migration to southeastern Nebraska. Eventually the Pawnee separated into four bands that scattered mostly throughout south-central Nebraska. The Grand Pawnee band settled on the Platte River. The Republican band settled on the Republican River in southern Nebraska and the Tappage group settled between the Grand and Republican bands. The Skidi Pawnee settled along the Loup River, a tributary of the Platte in central Nebraska. The Grands were considered the prominent band and the chief of this body made the decisions for the whole Pawnee Nation in matters of great importance.

The "Northern Pawnee" known as the Arikara, who eventually occupied stretches of the northern Missouri River, are believed to have been part of the Skidi band at one time, but it is not known when they separated and migrated north.

Judging from the lands occupied early-on by the Wichita and the Pawnee, it is not surprising that these were the people to make contact with the first white men to reach the Kansas-Nebraska border in the sixteenth century.

When the Pawnee first settled on the Platte, Loup and Republican Rivers, they lived in large villages made of straw or skin houses resembling the tipi which later was so popular with the nomadic plains Indians. At that time, they had almost full control of the area about them. Their only restrictions were on the west and north where the Comanche (Padouca) occupied the areas on the Dismal River. In these early times there was continual warfare between these two tribes. At a later time, the migration of the Arapaho, Cheyenne and Sioux pressured the Comanche to move to the southwest. The presence of these latecomers still continued to block the Pawnee from expanding to the west and north.

About the same time that the Arapaho, Cheyenne and Sioux were assuming their territories on the grasslands, the Omaha and the Oto tribes occupied sites along the Missouri River and the eastern stretch of the Platte River.

Shortly thereafter, the Kansa tribe moved into the area between the Kansas and Republican Rivers. Hence, even though the Pawnee occupied central and southern Nebraska very early, it wasn't long before other people greatly restricted Pawnee claims.

*   *   *

In 1516, the Spanish Crowns of Castile and Aragon were passed to Charles I and in 1519 he was elected Charles V, Emperor of the Holy Roman Empire. With this action, Charles became the most powerful leader in Europe and Spain had indeed become a world power.

Under Charles V, Spain developed a prime interest in carving an empire out of its colonies in the New World.

By 1521, after Hernando Cortes completed the capture of Mexico, he was appointed governor of that colony. Under his leadership, Mexico grew and prospered, but in his undertakings Cortes met great resistance from both the Indians as well as his own officers, who complained to Charles V about his manner of rule. In 1527, Cortes was ordered to return to Spain to defend himself against the charges of his accusers. Once back in Spain, however, he was treated kindly by the emperor who bestowed him with the title Captain General of New Spain.

Returning to Mexico in 1530, Cortes found that much of the treasure he had gathered had been squandered on unproductive expeditions by his fellow Spaniards looking for more wealth. He also found that his former authority had been divided up with much of it placed in the hands of others.

In 1535, Antonio de Mendoza arrived in Mexico as the first viceroy of New Spain and he took steps to rearrange the authority over the Mexican provinces. Among his most significant changes was his appointment of Francisco Vasquez de Coronado as governor of New Galacia with headquarters in Guadalajara.

The viceroy had heard stories from Indians about seven wealthy cities of Cibola that existed far into the interior of the unknown land to the north of Mexico. As a result, he commissioned Friar Marcos de Niza to visit these cities. When the friar returned from his exploration, he reported that he had seen one of the cities and corroborated the rumor about the riches of the area. Hearing this, Mendoza decided to seize all seven cities and he selected Coronado to form an expedition that would retrace the route of Friar Marcos.

When he heard of the appointment of Coronado to head the expedition, Cortes objected vehemently, but his complaints fell on deaf ears. Late in 1539, Cortes returned to Spain to take his protest to the Crown, but he never returned to Mexico again. Hence, the conqueror of Mexico lived long enough to see himself betrayed and to see that even in the Holy Roman Empire greed extended from one continent to another and prevailed over decency and loyalty to country.

It is an enigma that although the horse originated in North America as the three-toed, canine-sized, prehistoric animal referred to as "Eohippus," the first American Indians contacted by early explorers had no horses. It is almost for certain that the first mustangs obtained by the American Indians originally came from Spain, but it is not known when this occurred. These sturdy Spanish steeds, called "barbs," were descendants of the animals introduced into Europe by the Moorish invasion in 700 A.D. and they still possess the characteristic markings of their ancestors. They have greyish brown coloring, a dark stripe along their backs and zebra striping on their knees and hocks.

It has been written that the first Indians to obtain any large number of horses were the Shoshone, who acquired them from the Spaniards in New Mexico. Even earlier than this, however, it is known that the Comanche had horses and this allowed them to range from Mexico to the Canadian border in early times.

As stated above, the Pawnee and the Comanche were bitter enemies in Nebraska and it is held that the first time the Pawnee ever saw horses was when the Comanche rode them in battle against the people of the Platte. Shortly after this incident in the spring of 1539, Tatarrax, chief of the Grand Pawnee, met with his Council of Chiefs in the large Grand village on the north bank of the Platte. Aside from Tatarrax, the council consisted of the leaders of the Republican, Tappage and Skidi divisions. Essentially all of these leaders resembled their respective braves in their dress. All had closely shaved heads with scalp-locks at their pates. Tatarrax was clothed by a buffalo robe wrapped around his body with his chest and left arm bare. From his scalp-lock hung an eagle feather and his legs were protected with beautifully tanned leggings and moccasins.

The Republican and Tappage chiefs were dressed plainly in deer skins with no decorative items in their scalp-locks. The chief of the Skidi or Wolf tribe was dressed appropriately in the skins of the white wolf. His moccasins were colorfully painted and a red ornament dangled from his scalp-lock.

As Tatarrax opened the meeting inside the warmth of his large lodge, he spoke of the subject that was utmost on his mind:

"Fellow leaders, in our last encounter with the Comanche, some of you witnessed the presence of the animal the Comanche used against us in battle. I don't have to tell you that was the reason we suffered the losses we experienced. Even though the Pawnee Nation is the largest population in this area, we cannot afford to let the Comanche and our other enemies have this kind of advantage over us.

"The prisoner that we captured in this last fight has told me that his tribe obtained the big dogs called 'horses' from Indian tribes many, many miles to the south of here. We must obtain horses as the Comanche have done.

"I have gathered you here to ask your permission to travel to the south to look into the possibility of acquiring horses. I should also like to have my brave friend and fellow chief, Ysopete, go with me for support. I am sure that we will find such a trip to be of great advantage to the Pawnee in the future."

For Tatarrax to suggest that he engage in an exploratory trip in search of the horse was held as nothing unusual by the Council of Chiefs. It was customary for the chiefs of the Pawnee to assume dangerous, active roles as did their braves and was one of the reasons why the Pawnee fought so bravely in the presence of their war-chiefs. Hence, in taking a vote, the chiefs of all the divisions unanimously agreed to the adventurous probe suggested by the tough and intelligent Tatarrax.

Chapter II

The Zuni Connection

It was a balmy day in the summer of 1539 on which Tatarrax and Ysopete, equipped for the trail, moved on foot away from the Platte and in a southwesterly direction. Since they did not have the advantage of pack animals, the two chiefs traveled lightly with their weapons, buffalo jerk, sleeping rolls and moccasins their main items of supply. On this first day, the two chiefs made their way mostly through the tall grass of the prairie below the Platte. During the second day, however, the pair reached higher and rougher terrain indicative of the fact that they were approaching the Republican River.

The rough land encountered proved to be a salving factor on the third day of the trek. Late on this day, as Tatarrax and Ysopete walked along the bottom of a high, rugged ridge, they were suddenly surprised by two braves on horseback who pulled out on the trail from behind an eroded dune.

With axes in hand, the mounted warriors quickly converged on the walking pair. Recognizing the danger and with their wits about them, the Pawnee scrambled up the ridge taking refuge in a small cave near the top. Dressed only in loin cloths and horned buffalo caps and painted profusely with vermillion, the attackers looked up at the Pawnee. Having failed in their attack, the horsemen weren't about to try to extricate the Pawnee chiefs from their refuge. Frustrated, the riders whipped their steeds and sped off to the north.

Viewing the action from their high perch, Tatarrax and Ysopete breathed more easily and agreed that their attackers were Comanche. "This attack is a good example of how important the horse will be to our future," said Tatarrax. "If we do not get the horse soon, the people of the Platte will be reduced to a very weak power."

"From what I have just seen, it is essential that we are successful in our mission," stated Ysopete.

Since it was late in the day, the chiefs spent the night in their snug cave. At sunrise the next day, the Pawnee were again on the trail and before the sun was high in the sky, they sighted a Republican Pawnee village on the river. As the pair approached the massive collection of huts, they were welcomed by several grim-looking braves whose continual duty it was to look over the security of the village.

Quickly, the chiefs were whisked to the lodge of Tomak, sub-chief of the Republican Pawnee and the leader of this division of the tribe. After paying their respects to Tomak, the two leaders were taken on a tour of the settlement. Hundreds of homes occupied the north bank of the river in helter-skelter fashion. Life looked like it was good and the people seemed well-fed. Numerous buffalo hides were stretched in their racks and tanning in the sun. Children appeared safe and comfortable as they played and ran in groups. Occasional hunting parties trudged into the encampment with the hunters laboring under the weight of deer, antelope or elk. Here and there, small collections of braves sat discussing war or hunting experiences while the women of the village could be seen laboring in the fields tending to the maize, squash and turnip crops. All of this truly represented a sedentary lifestyle and was typical of all the villages of the hard-working Pawnee at the time.

Upon spending the night in the home of Tomak, the two Pawnee chiefs waded the river early the next day and again took to the trail across the grasslands of what is presently the western Kansas prairie.

The trek was hot, humid and exhausting. In order to conserve their strength, the pair did not travel in the heat of the day and made progress only in the cool of the morning and at dusk. They lived off of the land as much as possible, eating berries and small game wherever possible. Many times during their endeavor, they regretted having initiated it.

"This isn't the kind of life a chief is supposed to lead," said Ysopete one night as he pondered his fate. "Maybe some time in the future it will have been worth this sacrifice."

One day as the chieftains approached the Arkansas River, a thunderstorm came up suddenly. As the thunder rumbled up and down the river valley, lightening streaked all around them and the chance of a drenching rain became increasingly possible. Quickly, the chiefs spotted the opening to a large cave in the side of one of the river bluffs and they made a hurried dash for shelter. As they entered the cave, the pair concentrated too much on the relief afforded them to notice six heavily armed warriors standing at the rear of the cave. Before they realized what had happened, the braves disarmed them and made gestures for them to sit against the cave wall.

Immediately, Tatarrax noticed how much their captors resembled him and Ysopete. The shaven heads, the decorated scalp-locks and stumpy bows reminded him of a Pawnee hunting party and caused Tatarrax to sit in awe. "What do you intend to do with us?" queried Tatarrax in the straight Pawnee tongue. The question totally caught the attention of the leader of the warriors who recognized the linguistic style as that of his own.

"Of what tribe are you?" he asked.

"We are Pawnee," answered Ysopete, "and you must be our relatives of the Wichita Nation," he continued.

On those words the atmosphere in the cave became more relaxed as the Pawnee chiefs rose from their flexed position on the floor and greeted all of the Wichita braves.

Once the storm had passed, the Wichita braves invited the Pawnee to visit their village and meet their village leader. Tatarrax accepted and the two chiefs and Wichita braves proceeded down the Arkansas valley. It wasn't very long before a large village came into view that was composed of huts made of bark and animal skins. As the party approached, it was meal time and many fires burned in front of the lodges. The whole village had a smoky haze hanging over it as the party entered the settlement. The presence of the Pawnee caused no disturbance among the villagers mainly because they so closely resembled the Wichita.

In a short while, the party reached the lodge of Moltok and it wasn't long before the chief was standing outside and greeting the newcomers. "I am indeed honored to have such powerful leaders of our brothers, the Pawnee, visit the land of the Wichita. It is very unfortunate that it has taken us so long to be reunited," said Moltok. "What, may I ask, brings you to our valley?"

"We are en route to the south in search of the large dogs known as 'horses'," stated Tatarrax. "It is our feeling that we must acquire these animals in order to remain as strong as our enemies who now have them."

"Please come into my lodge," invited Moltok. "I would be honored if you would share my food and stay this night with me so that we might talk about horses further." Exhausted from the stresses of the trail, the Pawnee promptly accepted the warm invitation.

That evening, following some rest and a meal in the chief's abode, Moltok invited his guests outside and up the closest hill to the tribe's council circle. Here a considerable number of the Wichita braves were assembled along with a large group of highly decorated dancers. A very large skin drum was placed to one side of the circle and the three chiefs took some prepared seats opposite the drum and in front of a group of tribal dignitaries. The chiefs no more than took their seats than the drummer began beating out a cadence for the dancers. In a flash, the circle pulsated with costumes of many colors arrayed with even more colorful furs and plumage. The tribal medicine men danced in a group each dressed in rather dull garbs, but in very impressive buffalo caps. The whole exercise was indeed a memorable sight and one that Tatarrax and Ysopete would never forget.

As the drum beat picked up, shouts from all the shaven braves at the edge of the circle encouraged the dancers to pick up their rhythms as well. The celebration continued on and on until the dancers almost reached exhaustion. Then, as the dance and chants of the celebrants reached a common crescendo, the drum stopped and so did the dancers. The ceremony ended when a muscular medicine man, donning a buffalo mask and with spear in hand, emerged from among the dancers and drove the spear into the ground in front of the chiefs.

With this finale, the three chiefs and the Wichita warriors shouted their approval.

"This was the Wichita way of showing their appreciation for your visit," said Moltok to the Pawnee chieftains. "You see that they consider your presence a great honor." Tatarrax smiled and nodded his approval of the unexpected ceremony.

"After all this excitement, let us retire to my hut and discuss the subject of the horse further," suggested Moltok. Again Tatarrax nodded.

Once again in Moltok's home, the leader of the Wichita began: "The chiefs of the Wichita Nation have been concerned about the horse for some time now as apparently the Pawnee have been. We feel, as you do, that we must acquire this animal for our total survival. The question is: How do we do this?"

"We have found out from our enemy, the Comanche, that the horse has been secured from tribes far to the south. We are on our way to try to find or buy these animals and begin raising them soon," said Ysopete.

"We would like to be part of your quest," said Moltok. "I would be happy to assign some of my best warriors to go with you to give you assistance and protection."

"I believe that we will be safe without your warriors, Moltok. If we are successful in finding horses, we will let you know on our return trip," answered Tatarrax.

The reply by Tatarrax appeared to satisfy Moltok because it offered him an opportunity to find out more about the desired beasts without placing any of his people in jeopardy.

The next morning, Tatarrax and Ysopete bade goodbye to Moltok and again took to the trail for the southwest. On and on they traveled over smooth prairie and rough terrain putting many, many miles between themselves and the friendly Wichita. After several sleeps, the tired pair eventually reached the Canadian River and here they rested and bathed allowing their beaten feet and legs to heal.

Once back on the trail after crossing the Canadian River, Tatarrax and Ysopete found themselves in a very arid land and they realized as they walked that they would have to conserve water. Shortly, however, they reached the waters of the Pecos River. At this point, they decided to follow a more westerly direction and shortly thereafter they reached the Rio Grande. Here again they rested allowing their legs and feet to recover from the pounding of the dry, rocky soil.

After resting for two days, the two chiefs looked out onto nothing but desert beyond the Rio Grande. To them, it didn't seem to matter in which direction they looked or walked, because the terrain was all the same. Making sure that their water jugs were filled, the pride of the Pawnee Nation continued their trek to the west.

Day after day, the pair marched deeper and deeper into the hot wasteland not knowing whether to continue or retreat to the Rio Grande. Once their water supplies ran down, they realized that they could no longer pull back. They had only one choice...to move ahead.

One day, with the sun high in the sky, the Pawnee decided to take a break from the trek and rest in the shade of several tall rocks along the trail. Suddenly, with no warning, they found themselves surrounded by a hunting party of seven braves holding a variety of weapons.

The captors all wore loin cloths with accompanying kilts. Some were bare-chested and others wore shirts. The moccasins worn by these braves were made of soft deer skin and these were joined by cloth leggings of various colors and designs. Three of the captors wore necklaces made of silver and turquoise and one wore an earring made of the same material. The hair style of all the braves was the same with the hair parted in the middle, pulled to each side and either tied or braided.

The apparent leader of the group motioned for Tatarrax and Ysopete to get to their feet. Once standing, Tatarrax attempted to converse with his abductors, but his efforts were fruitless. The leader ordered his men to disarm the pair and once this was accomplished, he made gestures for the Pawnee to take the lead on the trail heading west.

After a long, hot trip over a rugged trail, the party began passing several large settlements. These consisted of many, large multistoried houses made of adobe brick or stone plastered over with clay mud. The dwellings had flat roofs and each story was terraced back from the one below. Upon marching past three of these settlements, the party stopped at the fourth, which was apparently the home base of the captors.

The abductors walked their prisoners to the middle of the city and here they placed them in a single-story building and locked the door from the outside. Tatarrax and Ysopete stood in shock for several moments pondering their fate. They were chiefs and had never been treated in this lowly manner.

Occupying the same room was another prisoner who had seated himself on the floor and against the wall. As Tatarrax and Ysopete spoke to one another, the other prisoner paid close attention as if he understood their conversation and at one point interrupted them.

"Of what nation are you?" he asked in the Caddoan tongue. Surprised at what he was hearing, Tatarrax was quick to answer.

"We are of the Pawnee Nation many miles to the north of here," he stated.

"I am Tawak and I am from the Caddo people who live along the Red River," offered the other prisoner. "I have been held here at Cibola for a long time and am considered a slave. I am forced to work in the maize and bean fields with the women to pay for my keep. If I didn't work, I know the Zuni would kill me. You too will probably be held as slaves."

"So these are the Zuni," said Ysopete "and these buildings must be the 'pueblos' that we have heard about from the Comanche. I never thought that I would meet the Zuni or live in a pueblo."

"Why do we speak almost the same language when I have never heard of the Pawnee Nation?" asked the puzzled Tawak.

"I believe that your people and ours were one many, many years ago before the Pawnee and the Wichita traveled to the north to occupy the grasslands and hunt the buffalo," answered Tatarrax. "Tales passed on by the elders of the Pawnee tribe state that we once lived in the valley from which you came. We may even have been part of the Caddo tribe at one time. The fact that the tongue has lasted all these years without change is indeed remarkable."

Soon the door to the cell opened and in stepped three braves of the hunting party who captured the Pawnee and a tall impressive Zuni with a colorful and woven blanket wrapped about his shoulders and body. One of the braves addressed Tawak and the Caddo slave answered him in the Zuni tongue. Apparently Tawak had been held at the pueblo long enough to learn the language of his captors and they were aware of it.

Tawak let the Zuni know that he could converse with the new prisoners, and, upon learning this, the tall Zuni gave Tawak a message for the Pawnee:

"Tell these prisoners that I am Alcar, war-chief of Cibola. Tell them that they are now slaves and will live here with you and do the same work as you in the fields. They will eat twice a day and they will not be allowed to speak to the women in the fields."

As Tawak relayed the message, Tatarrax became infuriated.

"Tell him that we are chiefs of the Pawnee Nation and that we are not to be treated as slaves. Tell him that making slaves of us would be reason for the Pawnee to war on the Zuni," shouted the Pawnee chief.

When Tawak translated the message to Alcar, the Zuni did not appear to be shaken. "Just tell the Pawnee to carry out their duties and they will have no problems," said Alcar as he put his nose in the air and stormed from the cell.

Apparently Alcar was unimpressed with what he had previously heard of the size and strength of the Pawnee and the people of the Platte.

Chapter III

The Turk

Appointed by Mendoza to explore and conquer the great land to the north, Francisco Coronado used the capitol of New Galacia, Guadalajara as the point for gathering his troops. In February of 1540, this city had never seen such a potent striking force as was assembling for the north-bound expedition.

Coronado, an attractive figure with a neatly trimmed beard and well-fitted armor, was a highly religious man totally devoted to the Spanish Crown. He was fully taken by the powerful and bristling army he had put together, because it was a force that one might expect on the bat-tlefields of Europe and not one to move on mere savages in the New World.

Second in command of the army was Captain Don Garcia de Cardenas, a typical, hard-nosed Spanish cav-alry officer who was hand-picked by Coronado. Aside from his responsibility as second in command, he headed up the more than two hundred armored cavalrymen. Aside from the horsemen, the troop also consisted of about one hundred foot soldiers armed with about every conceivable weapon. Among these weapons were the awesome crossbows and the traditional Spanish pikes which were reputed to strike terror in the hearts of adversaries.

Accompanying the army was a collection of Spanish priests including Friar Marcos, who had claimed to have previously visited one of the wealthy cities of Cibola. The presence of these members of the religious symbolized the desire of the Spaniards to convert heathen Indians to the belief in Jesus Christ and also to insure the blessing of the Church on any deed of the army whether in the realm of good or the realm of atrocity. Also, as part of the Coronado troop, were hundreds of Indians whose duties were to serve the members of the military and to care for the herd of spare horses which served both as mounts for the conquistadores and as pack horses for supplies and loot.

Adding to the color of the expedition were the camp followers...the women who had the temperament to straggle behind the movement of the men. These women were mostly Indians, but some were wives of the soldiers who preferred not to sit patiently at home awaiting the return of their men. In some ways, the expedition resembled the fierce armies of Ghenges Khan that ravaged Asia in earlier times.

Once the army received orders to leave Guadalajara, it proceeded to the sea and then north along the western Mexico coast. The temperature was cool as the force moved next to the ocean, but it became warm and then hot as the column turned inland. Day after day, the expedition trudged along in the heat and dust of northern Mexico.

At approximately one hundred days on the trail, Coronado led his men into the mountainous area of present-day Arizona. Here his troops and their animals began to show the effects of their arduous undertaking and many of the soldiers fainted from the labor of the climb and the heat. Here also the Europeans lost many horses that were not equal to the task. As a result of the food giving out, some Indians and a Spaniard named Spinosa died from eating what was believed to be water hemlock. At this point, it took much Spanish courage for the officers and men to continue on their mission, but one day a cool breeze from the north offered them relief and incentive to move on.

Eventually, the Coronado force dropped down onto a plain and crossed into what is western New Mexico today. During all of this time, the men were encouraged to continue on by Friar Marcos.

Suddenly, one day, the advanced scouts rode hurriedly into camp shouting that they had seen the cities ahead. On the next day, the Cibola city of Hawikah came into view of the total army. At this point, Coronado called together his captains, as well as Friar Marcos, to decide on strategy.

"Those walls and buildings give no hint of gold," said the general to the Friar.

"But the gold is inside their fortress," said Marcos in a feeble answer.

"Are these people friendly or will we have to conquer them?" queried Coronado as he looked directly at Friar Marcos.

"They were friendly to me because they recognized me as a man of God," stuttered the Friar, "but they will defend what is theirs."

"All right," said Coronado, "we will rest here tonight and in the morning we will see if they want to fight or not."

After the meeting, Captain Cardenas worked to ready his cavalry and foot soldiers for possible battle in the morning. In true Spanish tradition, the soldiers sharpened and readied their weapons for possible action.

In the morning, the young soldiers appeared eager for battle because it had been some time since they had been tested. Some had never tasted battle before.

Shortly after sunrise, Coronado gave the command to march on the visible fortress which was only one of the seven in the area.

Anticipating an attack from the approaching army, Alcar had his warriors positioned on the walls and buildings that composed the defenses of the settlement. These braves were armed with rocks, bows and arrows and deadly hatchets and war-clubs.

As Cardenas reached the wall with his cavalry and foot soldiers, Alcar stood up on his perched position and by shouting and using gestures, he indicated that he wanted the Spaniards to leave or he would fight. Coronado did not accept this and ordered Cardenas to commence with the attack. Arrows from the Spanish crossbows took down many of the Zuni warriors and the huge rocks hurled by the Zuni took their toll on the soldiers and horses below. The Zuni arrows, however, were mostly ineffective against the steel and leather armor of the Spaniards.

During the exchange of missiles, it appeared that the fight would reach a stalemate until the mounted fighters had the idea to stand on their horses and scale the distance to the top of the wall. Once the soldiers were positioned on the wall, the Zuni with their rocks and arrows were no match for the conquistadores wielding swords and daggers.

In the malay, both Cardenas and Coronado were injured by flying rocks, but before too long, Alcar decided to spare his braves and surrendered. Following the truce, Spanish soldiers who had gained positions on the wall opened the gates of the adobe fort. The whole army then marched into the pueblo city.

Coronado allowed the Zuni time to bury their dead and to conduct their usual ceremony for this event. This gave the friars time to hold a requiem mass for the fallen Spanish soldiers and also gave Cardenas and Coronado time to heal their wounds.

One day, when the troops were going about their regular duties inside the city and Coronado was resting in his tent, Alcar and an entourage of prominent Zuni approached the general's enclave. Hearing of the presence of Alcar, Coronado summoned Cardenas to accompany him to the meeting.

After salutations had been exchanged, Coronado found that he could not in any way exchange thoughts with Alcar or any of his party. The general then had the idea to send for Waté, leader of his Indian helpers. Once Wate' arrived, he found that the Indian leader could converse with Alcar through some words and gestures. This pleased the general because he felt he could clear up some disturbing questions.

Coronado invited the Alcar group to sit down on several camp seats that encircled the general's fire-pit. Turning then to one of his guards, he asked him to summon Friar Marcos. When the friar made his presence, the general asked Wate' to ask Alcar if he had ever seen the priest before. When the answer was returned in the negative, Coronado became furious with Marcos.

"You have lied to us all along. You lied to the viceroy, to me and to everyone else. You have disgraced the office you hold and you do not deserve to serve alongside these brave Spanish men. I want you out of my sight by nightfall. Take three horses, some provisions and several Indian helpers and leave for Mexico. If I return alive from this exploration, I will see to it that you are properly disciplined in the Church. I really should hang you now."

Not uttering a word and with bowed head, the priest turned and walked away from the others in disgrace. This was by far the lowest point in Marco's life and he was never to really recover from it.

The general turned next to Alcar. "Many people have told me that there is much gold in these cities. Where do you keep your gold or where are the mines from which it is obtained?"

"We do not have any of the yellow metal, nor do we know where it can be found," answered Alcar. "We too have heard of the cities built of gold, but we have never seen them. It has been said that they are many leagues north of here. Perhaps they are the cities of Quivira that lie within the Pawnee Nation."

At this point in the exchange, Coronado began to take a liking to Alcar because he felt he was telling the truth. His feelings were confirmed when the proud Alcar issued this further information. "We now have three slaves in our prison who may be able to tell you more about the shining metal. One is a member of the Caddo tribe and the two others are his relatives and members of the Pawnee Nation. They work in our fields, but you can visit with them when you wish."

On these words, Alcar and his party stood up and prepared to leave. Out of respect for the chief, Coronado stood and gave the Zuni a salute as they left the enclave. In his heart, the general had many regrets about the unfortunate battle that had occurred between the pueblo people and his army.

That evening as Coronado left his quarters in search of Captain Cardenas, he couldn't help but look across the broad wasteland to the south of Cibola. In the distance, he could see a small party moving across the moor heading for Mexico. Apparently the travelers were Friar Marcos and his Indian helpers carrying out the general's orders. Coronado couldn't help but feel a tug on his heart as he thought of Marcos, but he also hated a liar. He realized that an army is usually in enough jeopardy without the presence of a liar to create confusion and chaos. After all, the friar deserved every bit of the misery he was experiencing. He, and he alone, was responsible for the organizing of the expedition, the spending of a fortune to launch the probe and the loss of lives in the endeavor.

In meeting with Cardenas, it was decided that as long as the army was this far into the great unknown land that investigative trips should be made both to the west and to the east. It was decided that first Cardenas would lead a march to the west. This would give Coronado time to heal his wounds which were worse than those suffered by Cardenas. It would also afford Coronado time to make more extensive plans for a trip to the east.

It took Cardenas about three days to organize a group of distinguished cavalrymen and after mustering enough supplies to last a month, the small brigade rode in a direction directly west of Cibola.

The sun shone brightly the morning of the twentieth day on the trail. On this day, Cardenas sent scouts out in front of his column to attempt to spot the Colorado River which he anticipated to be in the area. It wasn't long before these scouts returned riding wildly up to the main group.

"Captain! Captain!" shouted one of the scouts, "we have just sighted a tremendous act of God. Directly ahead lies the most spectacular sight you will ever see in your life...a huge canyon of heavenly vision."

On these words, the rest of the brigade hurried their horses along to also view what the scouts had seen. Once on the rim of the canyon, the mounted soldiers gasped with amazement and no one uttered a word as the whole force contemplated the massive beauty. Standing on the edge of the canyon, they observed the silvery river far below and they marveled at the changing colors of this wonder as the sun bounced its rays off its vast, irregular walls. They had discovered the Grand Canyon!

That night Cardenas decided to camp on the rim of the canyon so his troops could absorb the beauty they had discovered. The longer the soldiers studied the canyon, the more they were awed by its rare sight. It was indeed the main event in their adventurous lives.

On subsequent days following the discovery, Cardenas set up a base camp on the south rim and then proceeded to make exploratory visits to various areas around the canyon...this to continue the incessant search for gold.

Meanwhile back at Cibola, Coronado arranged to have a meeting with the three prisoners of the Zuni. The meeting took place in Coronado's conference circle, which was a very active site in the planning for the trek to the east. In the meeting group was Coronado's Indian interpreter, Wate', the three prisoners, Alcar and Coronado. In the four-way exchange, Coronado asked Tatarrax who he was and where he had come from. Pointing to Ysopete, the Pawnee chief answered: "Ysopete and I are members of the Pawnee Nation. We come from many miles to the north of here. At present, we are slaves and we work in the fields which is an insult to us and our people."

"Do you know of the land of Quivira?" asked the general in an eager way.

"Quivira is the name for a large land which also includes part of that owned by the Pawnee," offered Tatarrax.

"Are there rich cities in Quivira containing much of the bright metal called gold?" queried Coronado.

"No, most of the cities are made up of skin and bark homes and we are only rich in good soil and buffalo," said Tatarrax. "I have traveled far in Quivira and there is no shining metal of which you speak."

"He has got to be lying," said Coronado to Alcar. "It looks like he wants to mislead us about the gold and keep us away from the area. Keep these slaves well guarded. We will need them as guides when we go east and possibly north." Alcar followed the orders and had the prisoners led back to their cell. Underneath, the pueblo leader felt very good because what he had just heard meant that the Spaniards would soon be leaving the city.

Following one month on the trail, the Cardenas party returned to Cibola with no tales of gold, but with plenty of tales of their marvelous discovery, the golden canyon of the Colorado River. Coronado, though responsible for the discovery, would never see it because his interest was not in exploration of sites of grandeur, but in the fame that would come from the discovery of golden treasures to the east or north.

Roughly in September of 1540, Coronado's hardened army and camp helpers left Cibola, this time guided by Tatarrax and Ysopete. As the large force moved in an easterly direction toward the Rio Grande, Tatarrax attempted to convince Coronado that his mission would end in failure and that there were no cities of gold in the land ahead. The words of the Pawnee chief fell on deaf ears because the Spanish general firmly believed that the rumors of the wealthy areas, that had circulated so far and for so long, had to be true.

To the Spaniards, the Pawnee and the Caddo did not represent any threat and they were allowed to mix with the rest of the Indian helpers. As Tatarrax, who was the most outgoing of the three slaves, became more and more familiar with the Spanish troops, they dubbed him "The Turk" because of his appearance with shaved head and scalp-lock. Nevertheless, Tatarrax accepted his nickname graciously and continued to try to be an influence on the haughty general from Spain.

By the time the army reached the Rio Grande, the cold winds from the north began to hint at what was to follow. So, when the column reached the pueblo of Tiguex, Coronado decided that he would use this city as his winter quarters.

With the general's decision, the army began its search for winter shelter in and around the pueblo. Hence, the soldiers and their helpers and followers occupied caves, dugouts and abandoned buildings in and near the village. In this regard, an empty group of adobe houses near the main village became very useful.

For company during the long cold days and nights, many of the calvary and foot-soldiers had their wives who had moved along with the army. The rest of the soldiers and helpers had to be content with company furnished by many of the female camp followers.

Coronado was fortunate to be able to occupy an adobe home in the main village, but despite his good surroundings, life became dull and uneventful as the weeks dragged on. Occasionally, one or two of the general's officers would call to report on the condition of the troops.

On the nicer days, the general would walk in his area of the village to keep fit and work up an appetite for the meals that his Indian cook, Pepata, would prepare for him. Pepata was a very heavy-set Zuni woman who had lost her maidenly charms many years before. Regardless, she was an excellent cook and a favorite of the general.

Pepata's appearance was one of the reasons why Coronado was totally surprised when one evening toward meal time, another Indian woman appeared at his door laden with supplies for the general's supper. Using a few words and gestures, she was able to convey to Coronado that his regular cook was ill and that she would assume the cooking duties.

The general was saddened to hear about his friend Pepata, but he soon lost thoughts of Pepata as he viewed the physical attributes of the new lady. She was beautiful and indeed an unusual sight here in the wilderness, thought Coronado. Immediately, he realized he had been away from civilization too long.

"I am Keeko," said the woman as she began her preparation of the general's meal. As Keeko carried out her duties, Coronado sat and admired her long black hair, fiery brown eyes and unforgettable smile. His manly urges were definitely stimulated by her shapely figure which was obvious even through her heavy, long robe. The general realized that he certainly wanted to have a different relationship with the young woman than what he had with his other cook, Pepata.

As the general sat at his table to eat, he invited Keeko to sit with him and share his food and drink. At first the lady appeared shocked because she realized it was not her place to associate with the general in any way. But, seeing the sincerity of Coronado, she gave the Spaniard a friendly smile and sat across the table from him.

The general's friendly side suddenly came to the fore. In this position, Coronado was not the general he had been for years and found himself attempting to entertain and attract the beautiful Zuni who made him feel very, very good.

After the meal, Keeko gathered her food and dishes and placed them into a large woven basket. After cleaning the table, she stood by the door and extended her hand to Coronado. He responded in kind.

Once Keeko had left the house, the general could not get her out of his mind. It had been a long time since any woman had captivated him in this way. He realized that as general, he controlled the lives and death of each of the soldiers and natives in the area, yet he could not understand why such a lowly servant should have such an effect upon him. All night long, the general tried to convince himself that he should not become attracted to this ignoble housemaid, yet he looked forward to the next day when he would see her again.

When the sun rose on the next day, Coronado found himself in an excellent mental state. Dressing, he left his home and proceeded to undertake his first inspection of his army's condition since arriving at the pueblo. All day long, the general met with his captains making decisions that might enhance the morale and living conditions of his men and their helpers. He admitted to himself that this was the first time he had been concerned about the welfare of the army helpers and he knew that it was only because Keeko was a helper.

As late afternoon approached, Coronado became excited as he thought about another visit by Keeko. With her in his mind, the general hurried through a visit with Captain Cardenas and then rushed home. At meal time, Coronado's eagerness for another meeting with Keeko was frustrated when she did not appear on time. Would she be coming or would Pepata be back to continue her duties? A knock on the door and the appearance of Keeko ended his fears and he greeted her with more enthusiasm than any conquistador had ever extended to a servant.

As the day before, Coronado sat and watched every move made by the gorgeous Zuni female. Following another delicious meal, the general attempted to become more familiar with her. In this endeavor, he was able to teach her more words in Spanish and to be more comfortable in his presence before she made her overtures to leave. Coronado did not pressure the lady into staying. He felt that would come with time and he also sensed that the lady had some warm feeling for him.

On the following day, after an excellent meal prepared by Keeko, the general of the conquistadores felt that he could not bear to have Keeko leave without letting her know something of his feelings for her. As she moved to leave his quarters, Coronado stopped her, took the basket containing the kitchen ware from her hands, and sat her down on a large seat near the fireplace. As he kissed her hand, Keeko made no attempt to resist his advances. She felt an attraction from the first day they had met and had longed for this moment.

It wasn't long before Coronado picked Keeko up from the uncomfortable seat and laid her on a soft animal skin close to the fire. Neither needed the fire to warm them and shortly thereafter, Keeko grabbed the general passionately and drew herself to him. Coronado was helpless. Where was the dignity of a Spanish general? Where were his thoughts of morality in this moment of temptation? These things did not exist and before long the pair had fulfilled the meaning of their love. Following this, both remained motionless totally absorbing the thrill of their deep feelings.

Caressing Keeko, Coronado had no feelings of guilt about his actions, because for the first time in his life he had felt real love for a woman. Neither Coronado nor Keeko wanted the evening to end so they remained in their embracing position for a very long time. Here in the quiet of the general's quarters there were no stifling military regulation. Here there were no social barriers—only the joy of intimacy between two willing persons.

As the hour became late, Coronado asked Keeko to remain with him the rest of the night, but the Zuni made him understand that she had to return to her parents who were also helpers to the army. The general understood and despite his complete love for Keeko, he watched patiently as she moved off into the night to join her family.

Keeko prepared several more evening meals for the general and each time she did, the pair renewed their love for one another. Within time, however, Coronado's maid Pepata returned to her duties. This meant that whenever the general and Keeko wanted to see each other, they had to meet by secret arrangement. Soon, however, the relationship between the general and the lovely Zuni was known to most within the village and the army camp. Eventually, the couple made no effort to hide the fact. No one, not even the friars in the camp, had the nerve to tell the general that his affair was beneath his station and that his actions were sins in the eyes of the Church.

CHAPTER IV

QUIVIRA

While still in winter camp, Coronado arranged to have several meetings with "The Turk." In these meetings, Tatarrax tried to convince the chief conquistador that no gold existed to the north and east, the direction of Quivira. Despite all of the talk at attempting to convince the general, Coronado's lust for gold was too strong to accept the words of Tatarrax, Ysopete and Tawak. Also, the Spanish general had a deep gut-feeling that the guides were covering up the truth about a gigantic treasure.

When the weather began to moderate in the spring of 1541, Coronado ordered his army to the Pecos River and descended its valley for many miles. Again he found no cities of gold or fabulous mine containing this metal. When Coronado felt he had explored the valley well enough, he made an abrupt turn to the east. Again marching for many, many days into the dry, arid wastelands, Coronado suddenly found himself engulfed in a system of canyons between the Rio Grande and the Rio Brazos Rivers.

Realizing that his army had been on the trail for a year and a quarter with no success, the astute general knew that morale was running low. At this point, he decided that he would split his forces. He decided to send a major portion of his expedition back to Cibola. He would then proceed to Quivira , directly to the north, with a hand-picked group of cavalry, a few foot soldiers, five priests, and Tatarrax, Ysopete and Tawak. This meant that most of the Indian helpers, including Keeko, would return to the safety of the seven pueblo cities.

In one of his meetings with Coronado, The Turk emphasized the following point: "Our people are friendly, so you need not worry about an attack from them. The Wichita are also friendly, but we might have some problems with the Padouca tribe once we leave the Wichita."

Again stressing the pointlessness of the probe into Quivira, The Turk offered these further words: "General, we are still very far from the Pawnee Nation and what you call 'Quivira.' I want to be truthful with you in that your efforts will all be in vain. I know the area of Quivira well and I have never heard of gold. All you will find are rivers, villages of skin huts and the buffalo grazing on the tall grass. The buffalo are a delicacy, but you will find no gold to whet your appetite. I am happy to be going home, but you will find that I speak the truth."

The general accepted The Turk's discouraging words graciously but he only smiled, continuing to distrust Tatarrax and the other Indians. At this point, Coronado demonstrated the grit of the Spanish by making plans to continue on in the face of adversity. This was one of the qualities for which the Spanish soldier was noted and one of the reasons why the conquistador held his dreaded reputation in the New World.

One day in the latter part of May, 1541 following the departure of the major part of the army to Cibola, the cut-down group of Coronado's force began its long trek to the north. When they reached the Red River, the Caddo, Tawak, approached Coronado. "General, this is the river that flows to my home east of here. I beg of you, give me my freedom to go home."

Many in the troop stared at the general wondering what he would decide in regard to Tawak. As the head conquistador sat on his horse gazing at the beautiful river, he spoke to Tawak. "I can understand why you would want to be free on such a beautiful river. You have been of great service to us in the past and I feel that you have never lied to us. This I respect. We will have The Turk and Ysopete as our guides, so go home to your Caddo people. Go with our blessing and carry the message of Christ to your tribe." On these words, Tawak became highly elated. He jumped in the air waving his arms and shouting Caddoan words of joy as he carried the news to the Pawnee chiefs.

It wasn't long before Tawak had his meager possessions packed and began his trek east along the river's edge, waving back to his Indian friends and his friends among the soldiers of Spain. Even Coronado smiled as he watched the former slave move down the valley and to the main desire of the human soul...Freedom.

The army crossed the Red River and headed across the present-day Texas panhandle. By this time, the heat of the trail became a very, very significant factor in the rate of travel and the open prairie, with lack of interesting landmarks, made the effort a very mundane undertaking. Eventually, the column reached the valley of the Canadian River and here Coronado decided to rest his men and horses for a few days. The pause was indeed appreciated by all including the Spanish officers who had been driving their men to the fullest.

Next to the silvery river that wound through the grassy prairie, Coronado meditated about this vast land, its emptiness, and his God who had led him here. He prayed and contemplated his fate. Certainly, this was the most frustrating situation in which a Spanish conquistador had found himself for some time. Should he go on?, he asked himself. Should he continue in the face of all the past failure? Was The Turk telling the truth and would he find just more open prairie and villages of skin huts? Coronado knew at this point that his only alternative was to continue on and face defeat, if that was his lot.

On and on trudged the tired units of the Coronado expedition. Into the heat of the blazing summer of 1541, they rode as they traversed the endless prairie of today's Oklahoma and Kansas. Just what price would the conquistadores pay for their conquest of the great American desert? Would their efforts be blessed because they were conducted in the name of Christianity?

One day in early July, the Spanish brigade observed the valley that Tatarrax recognized as that of the Arkansas River. He informed Coronado that he had visited this valley before and that the natives, the Wichita, were poor and friendly.

"On our way to Cibola, we visited the Wichita in a valley many leagues upriver," said Tatarrax, "They are relatives of the Pawnee and resemble us in customs and in dress. There is really no reason to visit them." Coronado agreed by nodding.

Again, Coronado ordered his men to make camp along the river telling them they would take several days to rest, heal and refresh themselves. This pause was a great relief for the trail-weary soldiers of Spain who took advantage of the break to clean and sharpen their weapons, tend to their horses, and forage for food.

The day before taking to the trail again, the Spanish general called for another meeting with The Turk. "Where is Quivira from here?" queried Coronado.

"We are heading directly toward the land of Quivira," said the Pawnee chief. "Once we leave the river, we may even see some of the people of that district who may be hunting the bison. You will soon see that I do not speak with a bad tongue and you will find no gold."

Still convinced that the gold existed and that Quivira would give him a clue as to where it was, Coronado explained: "We will leave here following a route toward the north star trusting in God to give us success in our search."

The next morning, the winding column of the Spanish endeavor began another surge on the last leg of its probe into the legendary kingdom of Quivira. Would anyone have believed at the height of the Holy Roman Empire that one day emissaries of this powerful dominion would be struggling on the desolate plains of the great American desert seeking wealth for its coffers?

Through the torrid heat of mid-summer, the sweaty, undaunted explorers moved through the flat grasslands of central and northern Kansas never once faltering or losing their Spanish dignity. Suddenly, on a burning day at the end of July, 1541, the party halted on the rim of the series of hills overlooking the Republican River. Scanning the valley below, the Spaniards viewed a rather large, smoky settlement on the north bank of the river. The village was made up mostly of skin and straw lodges with an occasional bark hut interspersed. Here and there a fire burned in scattered hearths throughout the village. Some smoke rose from the roof holes of a few of the homes and in front of some of the lodges, buffalo skins dried in their stretchers.

Without any delay, Coronado ordered his battle group down the slope to the water's edge. Then, he lead his people across the rather wide but shallow river and approached the village from the west. When about a quarter of a mile from the lodges, he called his men to a halt. The village looked almost free of male occupants and an occasional robed woman could be seen scurrying between lodges.

Coronado surveyed the village from his steed and many thoughts ran through his head. Certainly these crude homes did not reflect the fabled riches of Quivira!

The general called Tatarrax to his side. The Turk, who by this time was beginning to understand and speak Spanish quite well, rode up to Coronado's side on a strong but stubborn mule.

"Who is the chief of this village?" asked the general.

"I do not know the leader of this particular settlement, but these are Republican Pawnee and Ysopete is the chief of all the Republican people," answered Tatarrax.

"What lies beyond this place?" asked Coronado.

"Along this river there are several more villages like this. All are of the Republican Pawnee. North of here you will find the Tappage Pawnee and beyond that the land of the Grand Pawnee, the land with the largest population in this whole region."

The Turk did not tell the general that he was the chief of all the Grand Pawnee, preferring to keep that a secret and possibly using it to his advantage at a later time.

"Do you have some influence with the Tappage and Grand Pawnee?" asked the general.

"Yes, I have some persuasion amongst my people, The Grands, and also some among the Tappage," answered Tatarrax.

"Turk, I have decided to have my men rest here along this refreshing river. I would like you to have Ysopete explain to his people who we are and that we come in peace. Tell him that while we are here, he can live in the village. That way, we should have no problems with these unpredictable people.

"Also, I would like to have you ride north to the villages of which you speak and tell the governors of those areas that Captain-General Coronado of the kingdom of Spain requests their presence here for a conference. I will expect you back in a short while or we will come looking for you."

Tatarrax became somewhat angered by Coronado's forceful words, but he kept his feelings to himself because he realized that he was getting his freedom and that when he returned, he would be a slave no longer.

On the morning of the next day, Tatarrax was found on the trail north of the Republican village carrying out Coronado's orders. For this trip, he was allowed to use the mule given him by the Spanish soldiers and a bow and quiver of arrows presented him by the Indian helpers. The morning was very hot as the chief of the Grands plodded along on the mule. Only an occasional crow could be heard calling out on the prairie. About noon, Tatarrax spotted a hunting party approaching him from the north.

He suspected that it was some of the braves from the village he had just left.

Tatarrax did not hesitate and confronted the warriors that were obviously Pawnee, who were on foot and burdened with packs of meat from their hunt. Some of the braves who recognized Tatarrax welcomed him to their midst.

"I want you to know that your chief Ysopete and I have just returned from the land of the pueblos," said Tatarrax. "We were brought here as slaves by Spanish white men who are seeking gold. Ysopete is now in your village and the Spanish general and his men are camped nearby. Do not do anything to anger these intruders because they are mostly all on horses and have powerful weapons. Let Ysopete handle all of your dealings with them. He knows their language and understands them. I am on my way to bring back many Tappage and Grand warriors. We will then be able to confer with the Spaniards from a strong position. Stay in your lodges and do not attempt to steal their horses. That would be disastrous for the village."

Upon issuing these words, the Grand chief saluted the Republican braves and then rode off to the north on his mission that he felt would eventually free the Pawnee people from the greedy Spanish threat.

Following two sleeps on the trail, the Grand leader sighted a very large Tappage village on the Little Blue River as he penetrated deeper into what is present-day Nebraska. The chief felt comfortable and relaxed as he entered the village which was in his familiar surroundings.

To the Tappage Pawnee, Tatarrax represented an oddity, because never before had they witnessed a Pawnee riding a 'horse.' Large groups of villagers followed Tatarrax as he rode his mule up to the lodge of the Tappage chief, Hokar.

Viewing Tatarrax, Hokar rushed up to him and embraced him as a brother. "I am so glad that you are back from your search for the horse," exclaimed Hokar, "I see that you had some success. I hope Ysopete is safe as well. Come and rest in the lodge and tell me of your adventure."

That night, Tatarrax rested, feasted and related the full story of his great experience to the Tappage chief. He also received a promise from Hokar that when he returned for the meeting with Coronado, he would be joined by the chief plus two hundred and fifty of the first-line warriors of the Tappage people. For the first time in many months, Tatarrax relaxed into a deep sleep feeling fully secure about the future.

With the assistance of his sturdy beast, it wasn't long before the Grand chief approached the wandering Platte River in Central Nebraska, his native soil. As he halted his mule on the crown of a tall promontory overlooking his home village, he paused and meditated about his recent experience. Never did he imagine that it would develop the way that it did. In his mind, Tatarrax was relieved that he was home and free from the Spanish troops, but he knew that he had one more mission to carry out...that being to secure the freedom of his friend Ysopete and the Republican Pawnee from the grip of the Spaniards. He realized that the general of the conquistadores would have to be convinced that no gold existed in Quivira and that it would not serve his interests to fight the Pawnee.

When Tatarrax entered the vast village of the Grands, there was much merriment among the people because their chief had returned home and the mule indicated that he had made contact with people who raise horses.

After one day of rest, Tatarrax called an emergency session of his Council of Chiefs. Taking his time, he related all that had happened to him in his probe to the southwest and he pointed out the dangerous situation that faced the Pawnee with the presence of the Spanish brigade.

"We must impress the general from Spain with our strength, and by so doing, discourage him from any military action against our people," suggested the chief of chiefs. "The only way to do this is to move on him with about four hundred armed warriors. These, along with those promised by Hokar, will impress upon the Spaniards that we will not be intimidated."

The council immediately approved of the show of strength suggested by their head man and they indicated that they would be ready to move in two days.

At this point, Tatarrax prayed to the great Tirawa, thanking him for sparing his life in his great undertaking and for blessing him with the Pawnee people who were willing to fight and die protecting their own.

The open area around the Grand village had not witnessed such an awesome collection of fighting men before as it did on the day of the departure of the Pawnee to the south. Four hundred battle-trained warriors, with a whole array of weapons, stood on the prairie awaiting the order to march from the former Spanish slave. Huge skin drums beat out a cadence that lent courage to even the most timid of the savage-looking braves.

A huge roar went up from the large horde as Tatarrax took his position in front of the battle force seated on his mule. Never before was the Grand chief so proud of his people and his warriors, and with one motion of his arm, the bristling and stern-looking force moved through the tall grass.

Following three days on the trail, the Pawnee reached a ridge along the Little Blue River which overlooked the village of the Tappage people. Off to one side of the village could be seen another powerful assembly of warriors. From this, it was obvious to Tatarrax that Hokar was true to his promise to provide additional braves to the Pawnee cause.

On the order of Tatarrax to move to the village, the Grand Pawnee moved hurriedly down the slope to greet their Tappage cousins. Sheer bedlam broke out there on the plain and the distant hills shook from the roar resulting from the friendly reunion.

Viewing the activity from an elevated position, Hokar waved to Tatarrax who was struggling behind his men on his mule. As the two chiefs met, they showed almost as much enthusiasm as their men. It was probably the most spirited Pawnee gathering of all time and it was a great stimulus for morale within the Pawnee Nation. That night the camp fires burned very late and the Grands and the Tappage danced until some of the braves dropped from fatigue.

The older chiefs, totally incapable of keeping up with their braves, had the pleasure to a good night's sleep in the lodge of Hokar. In the morning, when they sought to rejoin their men, they could not believe the sight they saw. Over six hundred brawny braves were lying helter-skelter on the prairie in the positions they dropped in the celebration. Wisely, the chiefs decided to delay their trip by a day because they realized that their men would not be up to the strenuous challenge of the hot prairie. The Grands particularly appreciated the delay because it gave them time to recover from their arduous march from the Platte.

Chapter V

The Retreat

In the Pawnee village on the Republican, Ysopete kept in constant contact with Coronado trying his best to keep from offending him for he knew the Spanish brigade could easily defeat the warriors in the settlement if hostilities began.

On a warm morning in August, 1541, Tatarrax rode his mule into the Republican village followed by Hokar and two muscular Pawnee braves on foot. After riding through the town, the group was joined by Ysopete as they moved toward the Spanish tents. Once inside the Spanish camp, they halted close to Coronado's shelter awaiting his presence. Soon the general appeared and approached the harmless-looking group.

"Well, Turk! I see that you have followed my orders and returned in good time. Did you bring the governors of the Quivira areas north of here as I requested?" asked Coronado.

"Yes," spoke Tatarrax, "This is Hokar of the Tappage area and I govern the area occupied by the Grand Pawnee."

"You, The Turk, are one of the governors of Quivira?" questioned the general, "Why did you not tell me this earlier?"

"I felt that you may have thought I was a liar and had me killed," said the chief, "Now I can prove who I am."

Coronado was shocked at The Turk's words, but he knew that Tatarrax was not lying. Once Coronado regained his thoughts, he saluted the three chiefs one at a time and then suggested that they take seats and discuss what he had on his mind. From a standing position, the general addressed the three rulers of Quivira and Tatarrax interpreted the meaning of his words.

"This land including the fabled land of Quivira has been claimed by King Charles V of Spain. That means that all of the people of the Pawnee are his subjects and must obey his will. I, Coronado, am his emissary and will carry out his wishes. We know from reports carried to us by other visitors that Quivira is a very rich land with much of the yellow metal called 'gold.' As Quivira is now part of the Spanish kingdom, I am here to tax Quivira to help cover the costs of the kingdom. This means that you will be protected by the soldiers of the kingdom who will not allow you to be invaded by any other power such as other Indians or white men such as the French.

"I realize there is no gold here, but I want you Hokar and you Tatarrax to return to your villages and bring us the amount of gold that ten horses can carry. I would like to have you leave in the morning because time is important to us. We must return to Mexico before the winter winds begin to blow. The horses are ready and again I expect an early return."

The three Pawnee were totally surprised by Coronado's request and it deeply disturbed them. Tatarrax felt that he should speak for the others because he was the most familiar with the general.

"Great general, we feel that it is a great honor to be considered part of the Spanish empire and to be under their protection, but you are wrong. We Pawnee, inhabitants of Quivira, are rich in many things. We have much land, great rivers, and plenty of buffalo, but we have no gold. If we had it, we would give it to you because as you can see, it would do us no good.

"Ysopete and I feel that we are friends of the Spaniards. You treated us well...much better than our brothers the Zuni. I am not lying to you about the gold. If you wish, you may come with us to the great villages to the north of here, but you will find none of the riches you seek. We would enjoy a trip to the north with your men, but the Pawnee will not be enslaved or menaced by your soldiers."

On those words and on a signal from Hokar, a tremendous roar could be heard just over the hills to the north of the Spanish camp. Suddenly, without any further warning, a massive horde of Pawnee warriors appeared atop the hills for all to see. It was a frightening sight and sound as the braves clapped their weapons and stomped their feet.

For the first time in his life, Coronado felt both humility and alarm. It was simple for the veteran of many campaigns to see that his brigade would be no match for the powerful Pawnee striking force. In his heart, he felt relieved that he had not committed any transgressions against the Pawnee. At that moment, the great general was glad that The Turk was his friend and not an angry slave or enemy. Tatarrax understood Coronado's deep-seated feelings. He had certainly spent enough time with him on the trail to understand him. He understood that it was the general's duty to try to find the yellow metal for his king, but despite this, the Pawnee also had pride and would not be subjugated.

Again Tatarrax addressed the startled general: "General, even though we control the power at this time, I do not want you to think that I have lied to you. You are welcome to travel with us as we return home to see that there is no gold in Quivira. Now that we are all soldiers of Spain, we must be honest with one another."

Although deeply disappointed, Coronado fully believed Tatarrax and he could not help but be amused by The Turk's words. He smiled at Tatarrax and the other chiefs.

"I do not believe that it would do us any good to march to Quivira," said Coronado, "I believe you when you say there is no gold in the Pawnee Nation. The stories of the gold, that we believed, were false from the start. To show my appreciation for my Pawnee brothers, I want you to keep the ten horses I had chosen for the trip to Quivira. They are yours to use and to breed so that the Pawnee will have a good supply and remain strong against your enemies. This I hope will strengthen the bond between Spain and your people."

After issuing these words, the conquistador bade the chiefs farewell, promising to return another day. It is not known whether the general of generals would have been so companionable had he suspected that gold existed among the Pawnee. Retreating to his tent, the famous explorer contemplated his failures. Here he also made plans to return to Cibola and then to Guadalajara whence his colorful expedition originated.

The massive collection of Pawnee warriors set up camp near the Republican village in order to rest a time before returning home. In this period, they witnessed the Spanish brigade fold their camp and begin their long march to the south.

Several prairie wolves looked hungrily at the dejected column of Spaniards as it wound its way through the Kansas prairie in the scorching summer of 1541. Ironically, the troop followed almost the identical trail taken by the Pawnee chiefs, Tatarrax and Ysopete, at an earlier time. Little did these chieftains realize that their probe would be a contributing factor in the demise of a force the size of the Coronado army. Among all of the unfortunate things that resulted from their probe and the eventual Coronado expedition to the north, one benefit was derived...the obtaining of the horse, the initial objective of the Pawnee leaders. Thus, the Pawnee emerged as the only beneficiaries of the largest, most heralded and most highly financed expedition of its time.

Pawnee
The wide vast prairie was the only find
of the men with gold hysteria.
Tappage—, Grand—, and Skidi—kind
were the wealth of the famed "Quivira."

In the trek from the Kansas prairie to the pueblos at Cibola, morale ran very low. En route, the column moved very slowly and the soldiers, both mounted and on foot, discarded much of their armor and many of their weapons. It is said that the path taken by Coronado could be identified for many years by the trail of swords, daggers, helmets, breastplates and lances lying in the blowing dust.

When Coronado finally reached Mexico with only a remnant of his once proud army, he was disgraced wherever he went. Even though he fell into disfavor with the viceroy, he was able to resume his position as governor of New Galacia. But soon, in typical fashion of the Spanish hierarchy, another hero of the kingdom was banished by his peers and forced to live out his life in ignominy. Just as in the case of Hernando Cortes, the conqueror of Mexico, Coronado was pressured from his post and compelled to live in inglorious surroundings in Mexico City until his death in 1554. It would appear from the above that greed and only greed controlled the Spanish government system at the time. Bravery, service, sacrifice and accomplishment meant nothing to the Spanish lords. Gold, and the power of gold, were the underlying basis for fame and reputation masked in a fascade of the Spanish interpretation of Christianity.

CHAPTER VI

EARTH LODGE

Some time after the Coronado experience, Tatarrax stood on a high hill overlooking the very large village of the Grand Pawnee on the Platte. The chief contemplated the future of the Pawnee, and on this note, he was very pleased as he viewed the sturdy horses grazing on the grassy bottoms of the Platte tended by the young men of the tribe. These seed animals should form the nucleus of a future herd that will furnish a steed or two for every family in the Pawnee villages, envisioned the chief. Along with the fortune of owning these valuable animals was the responsibility of protecting them from raiding enemies, thought Tatarrax. So, in his mind, he planned the construction of corrals within the village where the horses would be kept at night.

In his meditation, the chief thought about his coming marriage to Pariki, a gorgeous Pawnee maiden he had known since childhood. What kind of a home would he build for her? It would have to be sturdy, dry and warm. While concentrating on the subject of homes, he thought about the adobe structures he had seen at Cibola. They were solid, warm and permanent...quite unlike the drafty, flimsy bark, straw and skin huts that the Pawnee were living in at the time. The chief thought about the many times the inadequate lodges were wiped out by the violent storms that hit the plains in both summer and winter. Would it be possible for his people to build a pueblo-type home? Could an adobe-type clay be found in the area to furnish the cement of construction? Tatarrax knew he would give the subject more thought.

The subject of good homes for his people did not enter the mind of the Grand chief again until a later time when the Grands were visited by a contingent of "northern Pawnee" known as Arikara. One day in a conference with Barigi, the head of the Arikara Council of Chiefs, Tatarrax asked about housing employed by the Arikara.

"We live like you do in houses built of buffalo hides and thatch," offered Barigi, "but since living along the great river to the east, we have noticed something of great interest in the building of the lodges. Apparently, long before the coming of the Pawnee to this, the land of the buffalo, another people occupied the hills along the great river. They must have had a great population because their villages existed for many leagues up and down the river. We do not know where these people have gone. It could be that they met with a great peril because none of them are left. We have looked at the ruins of some of their homes and we have seen some of the skeletons in their burial mounds.

"Their lodges were built partially into the ground and were made of great timbers, soil and sod and there was room inside for many people and a great warm fire. They must have been comfortable dwellings."

Barigi's words excited the curiosity of the Grand chief. "Maybe we could learn a great lesson from these ancient people," roared Tatarrax. "It is late in the year now, but when the warm weather returns, I should like to see these ancient homes of which you speak."

"You are welcome to the villages of the Arikara along the great river whenever you decide to honor us," said Barigi.

The description of the ancient lodges along the Missouri River stimulated Tatarrax to the fullest. This was possibly the break the chief was looking for in his quest of the ideal permanent dwelling for the Pawnee.

The winter of 1541 was a very severe one and the activities of the Pawnee tribes were restricted merely to maintaining the necessities of life. Occasionally, at breaks in the weather, hunting parties would bring in fresh supplies of meat, which were a treat from the dry and salted buffalo jerk that composed the diet of the Pawnee during most of the winter.

One advantage of the bitterly cold winters lay in the fact that the Comanche were less active and did not harass the people of the Platte as they did during moderate temperatures. During cold months, the women of the tribe would congregate at one lodge or another and spend their time making or repairing items of clothing and footwear while gossiping about village affairs and people. This is the time also that the young braves were forced to sit with the older men of the tribe and listen to exaggerated tales of hunts, wars, and coups of times long past. Winter was indeed the time of the heroes of long ago.

The cold weather was also the time when a young man of the tribe had time to court the lady of his choice. Most courting was confined to the lodge of the girl's parents and the number of visits by a young suitor was usually restricted to three or four a month. Good weather was better for couples contemplating marriage because they could spend time walking in the village and talking with more privacy. Courting was not a frivolous activity among the Pawnee and it was not allowed unless both parties approached it seriously.

Tatarrax was allowed to visit Pariki more than usual, not because he was the main chief, but because he had already given his promise to marry the dark-eyed beauty. The chief was greatly respected by the girl's family because they realized that Tatarrax would take good care of Pariki and give her a good home.

Once spring arrived in 1542, Tatarrax and Ysopete were found on the trail to visit the Arikara settlements along the Missouri River. As the pair moved east along the Platte valley, travel was easier than when last they launched an exploration together. Tatarrax rode the mule given to him by the Spaniards and Ysopete rode one of the gallant steeds presented to the Pawnee by Coronado.

The venturesome chiefs pushed themselves very hard since they felt that they were on a very important mission. Following five sleeps, the pair reached the wide Missouri. From a high point overlooking the waterway, the Pawnee leaders gazed with total surprise at the beauty below. Never before had they seen a valley and a stream of this magnitude. So impressed were the Pawnee with the view that they witnessed, they decided to camp, rest their bodies and enjoy the spectacular scene for two days.

Once on the trail again, the pair moved north along the river. In following the waterway, they moved through an entirely different kind of terrain than experienced along the Platte. The hills and bluffs made travel more difficult than what they were used to on the flat bottoms of the stream that wanders across the total of the Nebraska plain. Following several days, the chiefs suddenly found themselves overlooking a large village on the west bank that they assumed to be one of the great settlements of the Arikara tribe.

Without hesitation, the Pawnee rode into the encampment and headed directly to the chief's enclave. Tatarrax and the Republican chief hadn't even dismounted when they were greeted by their friend Barigi. Ushered into the warm hut of the Arikara chief, the Pawnee enjoyed comforts around a flickering fire. It had been a long, stressful, chilly trip and the chieftains lounged on a set of buffalo robes with no immediate desire to exert themselves. Barigi recognized this and suggested that the tired travelers relax and think of serious matters later.

When two days had passed and the Pawnee had regained their strength, Barigi visited with them in the lodge reserved for honored guests.

"In the morning, I want you to accompany me to an area north of here along the river. This is the place that I told you about earlier that was one day settled by an ancient culture which are not our ancestors. I think we should spend some time studying some of the house ruins there," remarked Barigi. "You will be surprised and very interested."

Early the following day, the three leaders walked through some very thick underbrush and up an over-grown trail to the top of a very steep hill which overlooked the river valley. On the summit, Barigi led the Pawnee to a rather large depression in the ground. This depression was almost perfectly circular and formed a cavity that was as deep as a man's chest below the normal flat surface of the hilltop.

It was obvious to Tatarrax that the Arikara had shown a great deal of interest in the depression from the two trenches they had sunk in the pit.

"Our digging has shown us that at one time this was a large dwelling," said Barigi. "The people who built it first dug a large, round pit in the ground. They then burned down trees to obtain large timbers that they placed upright in holes in the bottom of the pit around its edge. They also placed four taller poles in a square toward the center of the pit floor. The builders then attached all the poles at the top with lateral timbers and then the outer timbers were joined with the center supports by large rafters. All timbers were tied at their joists to form a solid framework. Over the total structure, the builders laid sod and earth to produce thick walls and a domed roof. A large fireplace was built in the center of the floor and a hole was put in the center of the roof to carry off smoke of the fire. The entrance was built in a manner the same as the house and always faced to the south to avoid north winds.

"The houses built by these early people were warm in winter and cool in summer and were very permanent. They were large and each held two families or more. I think if we could build lodges similar to the one that was here many, many years ago, it would afford great comfort to both the Arikara and the Pawnee."

Tatarrax looked at the large size of the pit, still evident on the surface, and tried to imagine how the lodge appeared hundreds of years before. It was mind-boggling to the chief to realize that the product of an ancient architect may once again grace the encampments of the Great Plains.

In the one visit to the ancient site, the Pawnee chiefs felt that they had obtained enough information from Barigi to be able to construct similar homes. They were anxious to carry the news to their villages and to begin projects of their own. Hence, they left the good company of the northern Pawnee earlier than anticipated and began their journey back to the Platte.

Once they arrived at the Grand village, Ysopete made plans to return to his Republican tribe, but Tatarrax returned to a very serious problem. In his absence, the Grands had received word from the Skidi people on the Loup River that the Comanche had begun a strong harassment of their people. In the absence of Tatarrax, the elders of the tribe voted to go to the aid of the Skidi with a large band of Grand warriors under the command of Dako, a young, brave war-chief with great devotion to all of the Pawnee people.

Tatarrax thought that the elders had made the right decision, but even though very tired from his trip, he felt that he should join his warriors and his cousins, the Skidi. For this journey, Tatarrax picked a strong, rested steed of beautiful coloring and he put his over-worked mule out to pasture for a long-deserved rest.

Following two days on the trail, the Grand chief approached the motley-looking settlement of the Skidi. Oh, thought the chief, how a series of earth lodges could better the appearance of the place.

All appeared peaceful to Tatarrax as he rode into the village and up to the hut of Pitulk, chief of the Skidi. Tying his horse to the chief's pole, he rapped on the entrance support of Pitulk's home. He was soon greeted and invited inside where the two leaders discussed the problems at hand.

"Ever since the good weather moved in, the Comanche have been attacking some of our camps on the Middle Loup. They have killed four of our warriors and wounded several more. They seem to be more mobile than they used to be because they have more horses," offered Pitulk. "I don't know how to protect our people who are so spread out."

Tatarrax answered wisely: "We have now obtained some horses like the one I rode here and it will not be long before they will multiply into a great herd. I think that it would be wise for the Skidi to move down the Loup to be closer to the Grands for a few years until we can improve our warrior forces with the help of the horse. Right now, all of the Skidi are too vulnerable to the Comanche attacks. If all of your people would move down river, we could consolidate our defenses and our striking forces. If you continue the way you are now, you will just become weaker and weaker. If the Comanche want to attack us after you have pulled back, we will cut them to pieces."

"You are right, Tatarrax," said the Skidi chief. "I will give the order to all the Skidi people to begin the move tomorrow. I hope you will leave your contingent of warriors here to help my people in this effort."

"The Grands are in good shape and we do not need the help of those braves at the moment. I will speak to Dako to tell him to give you all the help and protection you need," said Tatarrax.

The next day, the Grand chief took to the trail to return home, for he was anxious to begin his earth lodge home which would be his present to Pariki. About mid-afternoon of the first day on the trail, as he moved through a wooded area along the Loup River, Tatarrax was suddenly surprised by five Comanche braves on foot. Immediately, the warriors attacked the chief, firing a shower of arrows and hurling several long lances in his direction. Tatarrax quickly turned his steed and in a flash was carried safely away from the marauders who were intent on his demise. Once again heading in the direction of the Platte, the chief felt sympathy for the Skidi who were subject to Comanche attack almost daily. He was also thankful that the Comanche were not totally equipped with horses, which one day they would be.

Chapter VII

The Culture of the Platte

Although tough and fearless in battle, the Pawnee were more sedentary than some of their neighboring tribes, such as the Comanche. The Pawnee villages were rather permanent and in the spring of the year, the people, particularly the women, would plant large areas of maize. This crop composed the major part of the diet of the Pawnee save for the meat of deer, antelope, elk, and buffalo. The Pawnee hunted deer, antelope, and elk during most of the year, but the buffalo were only hunted twice a year on large hunts that would take most of the tribe into the grassy sandhills north of the Platte River. These hunts were very significant to the people of the Platte because they not only furnished the major meat supply for the food coffers in summer and winter, but the hunts also furnished the hides for clothing and shelters.

In planning the site for his earth lodge, which was to be his home after his marriage as well as a model home for the entire tribe to copy, Tatarrax chose a high point some distance from the flood plain of the river. Enlisting the help of his brother Atego, Tatarrax began the excavation task, the first step in the construction of earth lodges. The digging was difficult work for both men as they used hoes fashioned from the scapulas of buffalo to remove earth from the pit.

Following the digging task which took almost a month, the two workers began the job of digging post-holes in the floor and burning down trees to supply the timbers. Once the framework of the lodge was built, the pair took on the task of digging sod to pack up and around the structure. When the sod was in place, the spaces in the sod were filled in with soil. The final step in the construction was the digging of a large fire-pit in the center of the floor inside the house within the four main center supports. As a final task, the religious pair built a small, elevated altar or shrine to Tirawa along the north wall in a gesture of thanksgiving for giving them the needed structure.

From an outward appearance, the lodge was dome-like with a long, flat entrance or porch. It was indeed a novelty to the Pawnee people who viewed it and none could criticize it from the standpoint of stability and comfort.

In the weeks that followed the construction of the chief's home, other families in the village began similar projects. Similar construction also began in the villages of the Republican and Tappage Pawnee. When the Skidi arrived on the Platte, they also started construction of earth lodges instead of building a whole new settlement of skin and bark huts.

Plans for the wedding of Tatarrax and Pariki were made for late in the summer of 1542. The site for the ceremony was to be the earth lodge constructed by the chief and all of the important people of the Grand, Tappage, Republican, and Skidi tribes were invited to participate. With the announcement of the wedding, most of the women of the Grands began elaborate plans to make the celebration a memorable occasion. Their main responsibility was the preparation and serving of food to all guests and members of the tribe. Each individual took the responsibility to prepare the finest of dress or costume for herself or himself. Those individuals who would be involved in the various dances of the celebration put forth an extra effort to decorate their costumes with colorful feathers, hides, and other decorative items.

The valley of the Platte was a veritable beehive of activity on the day that the Grand chief and his lady were to make their promises of marriage. Tatarrax looked tall and handsome in his long robe of office. Pariki was a beautiful sight to behold in her white beaded dress and with her long, black hair bound in a long strand on each side of her head. She truly was the finest beauty in the whole area of the Platte and deserving of the love of the finest man in the Pawnee Nation. The actual ceremony of the union, in true Pawnee custom, was a very private affair. Aside from the members of the two families, the only other people attending were the distinguished chiefs of the other Pawnee tribes who would serve as witnesses.

Pariki and Tatarrax stood in front of Pariki's father holding hands, the symbol of marriage union. The father then lit the sacred marriage pipe which was adorned with eagle feathers indicating strength, security, and permanence. Once he had smoked the pipe, he passed it to Tatarrax to smoke and then to the witnesses. With this completed,

Tatarrax then stood and announced for all to hear that he pledged himself to provide for his bride's safety and needs until his last day. This concluded the ceremony and afterwards the families and guests issued their congratulatory remarks to the newly married couple. As a final step to the ceremony, the chief and his bride left the privacy of his lodge and began receiving tribal members who were anxiously waiting outside.

At the first sight of the couple, the massive collection of Pawnee began their celebration. The valley of the Platte had never before seen a celebration of this magnitude because everyone loved the couple and wanted to be a part of the festivities.

The large skin drums that were set up here and there though out the village began to rumble out a beat for those who cared to participate in the Marriage Dance. No one lacked food, and in some cases, people gorged themselves into discomfort. At night, huge fires were built at various places in the village and the reflections of the fires in the water of the Platte were an amazing sight to see.

Many of the celebrants carried on long after the newly married couple had retired and in the morning, many could be found still celebrating in the manner as the night before. Even though many of the distinguished Pawnee had over-indulged, the celebration was good for the morale of the tribe that had not celebrated in this manner for several years.

At the next regular meeting of the Council of Chiefs, following the scheduled agenda, a young Grand sub-chief named Buksa asked to address the council. Upon receiving permission, the bronzed, haughty warrior stood in his position and issued these comments:

"Great chiefs, it is my opinion that we, the powerful Pawnee, are wasting time that we will regret some day. Ever since early spring, we have been harassed by the Comanche. Even the Skidi have had to retreat to the protection of their fellow Pawnee. To me, this is very humbling and it will only lend encouragement to these marauders. We, the Pawnee, are too large and strong to be dishonored in this way. I feel it is time we move on these scavengers and send them back into their hills mourning their dead. If this council will give me permission, I will organize a striking force among our four tribes and teach these Comanche a lesson they will remember forever. I can see no purpose in just sitting here and letting them prey on our small villages from now on." In concluding, the muscular sub-chief took his seat still showing a concerned and grim expression on his fierce face.

Pitulk, the chief of the Skidi, was the next to stand and continue the subject introduced by Buksa:

"We, the Pawnee, are fortunate to have warriors such as this magnificent, young Grand chief. It makes me very proud that the young men, such as him, are willing to fight to protect our villages. No other people know the scourge of the Comanche more than we, the Skidi, who have been their target for more than a year. We have lost many people and have had our villages burned. I am definitely in favor of striking back by turning our young braves loose to carry the war to their camps, but I do not know if this is the time for this kind of warfare. I would like to hear the opinion of others on this matter."

Tatarrax rose impressively to give his opinion on the subject:

"Fellow chiefs, I listened with great interest to the words of Buksa and naturally I am very sympathetic to the trials suffered by the Skidi, but I do not believe that this is the time for open warfare. We know that the Comanche have horses, but I believe that we have more because of the gift from the Spaniards. We should be able to raise horses faster than the Comanche and in time we will have an advantage over them in numbers. If the Comanche are still active when we have a good supply of horses, I too will be in favor of taking the fight to their camps. In the meantime, we should protect our horses and prepare ourselves until we are strong enough to attack in a convincing way."

The old chiefs appeared to agree with Tatarrax, but the younger men, particularly Buksa, just glared at the older men in disgust as the meeting adjourned.

Despite the wishes of the older, less impulsive Pawnee chiefs, the people of the Platte did not have to wait long to prove themselves to the Comanche. In the fall of 1542, it was decided in the camps of the Grand that a buffalo hunt into the hills to the north of the Platte was necessary to supply the food stores for winter. As was the custom of the tribe, the chief directed the hunt, but not as much religious significance was attached to the gathering of buffalo meat as with many other tribes of the plains. However, much preparation was needed to be carried out by the families who would participate in the ordeal. Food had to be packaged, weapons needed to be prepared or repaired, portable shelter needed to be prepared and proper clothing and footwear had to be made for this great endeavor. Consequently, from the day that the hunt was announced to the day it started, The Pawnee worked diligently to be ready.

As director of the search for bison, Tatarrax figured that the horses the tribe owned would play an important role. The chief decided that the horses would only carry the meat obtained by the hunters on foot. However, he felt that if the hunting proved difficult, the horses could be used in the slaughtering of the bison.

It was a time of excitement for the young hunters of the tribe who had never before hunted buffalo and this excitement grew as the cavalcade of meat-seekers left the Grand village on the Platte and headed into the sandy grasslands to the north. The hunt director estimated that it would be about a three-day trek before it was possible to sight buffalo, so in this time no scouts were sent out to locate the bison.

On the third day in the hills, when the tribe was making plans to camp for the night, Tatarrax sent out six young runners to try to locate buffalo. These runners fanned out to the west, east and north. Just before sundown, two runners returned with news that a large herd was seen grazing about two miles to the northwest.

All of the young braves who were hunting novices, could hardly sleep that night anticipating the thrill of their lives. Even before sunrise, many of the eager hunters gathered at the tent of Tatarrax for instructions. Here the chief passed out hides of wolves and buffalo under which the braves would hide in order to close on the grazing animals. Even though this practice had been successful in the past, it was a dangerous procedure because if the animals stampeded in the wrong direction, there was the great chance of being trampled.

Once the total hunting force had gathered, they moved slowly in the direction of the herd followed by the women of the tribe who would butcher the fallen beasts and wrap the meat in packs made of the hides taken from the animals. Behind the women, several young men led horses pulling travois onto which the meat packs would be loaded.

As the hunters approached the herd, it was obvious that it was made up of at least two hundred animals. The animals appeared very docile as they fed in a small dale encircled by low, rolling sandhills. Tatarrax gave his hunters instructions to surround the herd on three sides and after the braves donned their respective furs, they began the long, tedious job of approaching the wary beasts. The slow-moving hunters in their crude disguises did not appear to frighten the bison who only showed interest in the tender grass.

Closer and closer crept the Pawnee braves who clutched their bows and arrows as they crawled on their hands and knees. Suddenly, on the left side of the beasts, one of the braves in the hide of a wolf stumbled in his movement forward. This startled the closest animal and in a flash the herd began to propel away from the surrounding Pawnee. It was an awesome sight as the thundering herd began to build momentum into their stampede. The hunters needed to move swiftly as they saw the buffalo move away. Quickly, they rose to their feet and began pumping arrows into the bulls that raced by. Some of the missiles found vital spots on several of the big hulks sending them crashing to the ground in massive heaps. In but a moment, the herd was gone, leaving the plain dotted here and there with large brown carcasses. Once the dust had settled back onto the grass and sand, the women began their difficult job of dissecting the edible meat from the large mounds of hide and hair. Before the end of the day, the Pawnee had several of the travois behind the horses loaded with packs of meat and the hunting party returned slowly to camp.

The next day, the women of the tribe spent the day drying and salting the meat and scraping the hides that would wrap the prepared meat for the trip home. The younger men spent the day bathing and playing in the nearby creek while the hunters, who were above performing the mundane tasks, spent the day in conversation comparing notes on the hunt.

The hunting party, under the guidance of Tatarrax, spent several more days gathering meat and when all of the travois were filled, it began the long, slow trek toward the wide Platte valley. The meat harvest proved very satisfactory and was close to being as bountiful as any other hunt conducted in the sandhills. The presence of the horses reduced the labor for all in the party and for this they were very grateful.

Chapter VIII

Comanche

Of all the activities involved in the relationship of American Indian tribes, the most perplexing were the feuds that occurred between them. Many times these feuds developed between people of the same linguistic stock, and many times wars broke out between tribes despite the fact that there was plenty of land and food for all. The antagonism between the Comanche and the Pawnee was of the latter kind since these tribes were the only occupants of the whole of what is present-day Nebraska.

Laden with the meat harvest, the Pawnee cavalcade moved south out of the Nebraska sandhill hunting grounds. Since most of the tribe traveled on foot, it was a slow, mundane trip with each able person carrying bundles of weapons, food and shelter material. Tatarrax, the hunt director, only moved his column when he had scouts roaming out ahead and to the side of the hunting party. The load carried by the Pawnee was no secret to roaming

packs of wolves and coyotes who spent many hours following the sluggish cavalcade.

During the third day on the trail, scouts were
dispatched as usual, but when the front runners had
traveled about three miles ahead of the party, they turned
and retreated back toward the column. As they ran, they
tried to get the attention of their tribesmen by waving their
arms wildly. In accomplishing this, the cavalcade was
ordered to a halt and Tatarrax ordered his people into a
defensive circle to get ready for an emergency situation.
When the scouts reached the circle, they notified Tatarrax
that they had sighted a formidable war party directly in
front at a distance of about four miles. Soon the scouts
from all directions returned and the warriors began
breaking out their weapons and forming a protective shell
around the women, children, and animals in the circle. In
just a short while, the Pawnee had formed a strong,
bristling, and fearsome defense.

Before anyone in the circle could relax, Tatarrax spotted
an approaching battle group that he identified as
Comanche. Drawing closer, the Comanche war chief studied the tough defensive knot ahead of him. He could tell
that the Pawnee braves equaled him in number. After a
moment of thought, he decided to test the heart of the
braves in the defenses. Waving his lance in the air, the
brown, muscular war chief then pointed it at the Pawnee.
On this, the two hundred battle-experienced Comanche
raced toward the defense circle.

The Pawnee braves, seeing the advancing Comanche,
readied their weapons and braced themselves for hand-to-
hand combat. As the attackers came into range, three of
them went down from arrows launched by Pawnee

bowmen. Waving axes and war-clubs above their heads, the Padouca slammed into the motionless Pawnee. Immediately, individual duels developed between knife-or axe-wielding fighters of both sides. Feelings of horror broke out among the women and children within the circle as the opposing sides clashed. Screams of the women and children mixed in with the death screams and grating sounds of clashing weapons. As the battle ground on, the sand and grass of the prairie became red and brown with the blood and bodies of both sides. It was a frightful sight and the hills rocked with the horrific sounds.

After a time, it was evident to the Comanche chief that he was not going to crack the hard shell created by the well-conditioned Pawnee dog soldiers. He began passing a message among his braves and soon the Comanche started falling back. When contact had broken off, the Comanche withdrew to a hilltop overlooking the warriors from the Platte. Many thoughts crossed the chief's mind as he viewed the bodies of some of the Comanche lying face down in the sand in front of the Pawnee defense. Seemingly confused about his next move, the war-chief studied the situation below. He now faced the dilemma of possibly suffering defeat or losing face. Once his warriors had reorganized, the fierce leader appeared to think more of the Comanche pride than the lives of his men. Shouting his orders from in front of a long line of braves, the chief raised his long spear. Then, with one forward thrust of his arm holding the lance, the Comanche battle force lunged forward again toward the Pawnee.

Still at the forward position with his men, Tatarrax could see that the Comanche chief was leading the second attack. Immediately, Tatarrax shouted that he wanted to face the Comanche chief alone. Again the sounds of the clashing shook the neighboring hills. The Comanche chief seemed shocked as Tatarrax stepped in front of him to halt his forward progress. Instantly, the chief used his lance to block the tomahawk wielded by Tatarrax. As the battle raged around them, the two leaders hacked and stabbed at each other in desperate motions. During the struggle, the long shaft of the Comanche's lance broke under the pressure of the Pawnee chief's sturdy ax. Cooly, the Comanche reached for a huge knife in his belt and the deadly contest continued. The slashing of the knife opened the skin on Tatarrax's side and small amounts of blood began to trickle down his leg. This angered Tatarrax and spurred him into a greater effort to put the Comanche away. Chopping furiously at the Comanche chief's arm holding the knife, the Pawnee soon knocked it to the ground. Then lunging at the Comanche, he forced the marauder off his feet and killed him with a sharp blow to the side of the head.

In the furor of the fight, it wasn't long before the attackers realized that their chief had gone down. Suddenly befuddled and disordered, they withdrew from the melee. Under the orders of Tatarrax, the Pawnee cut short their pursuit of the retreating marauders allowing them to pull back into the hills of sand.

The fighting force of the Pawnee, witnessing the retreat of the Comanche, had mixed feelings about the results of the battle. Some whooped it up celebrating the victory over the undaunted enemy. Others looked about sadly as they viewed some of their fellow tribesmen lying dead in the grass...the price paid by the Pawnee for defending their rights to the hunting grounds in the grasslands.

The Pawnee decided to give their dead heroes a proper burial. Ordinarily this tribe wrapped their dead into death bundles and placed them in trees or on a wooden platform above the reach of scavengers of the prairie. However, because no trees or wood existed at the site of the battle, the tribe made the decision to bury their dead. The rest of the day was spent placing the Pawnee heroes in the sand. It was a distressful time for the unfortunate Pawnee families and for the surviving braves who held to a close brotherhood with their fellow fighting-men.

Tatarrax thought about the men that the tribe had just given up. Kubak, Buksa, and Wadki were just a few of the brave men that were lost. Oh, how he would miss the intelligent and bold Buksa!

The people of the saddened tribe did not take time out to bury the dead of the Comanche, preferring to leave them as sustenance for the roving predators of the plain.

When the tribe finally reached the Platte, little activity took place in the Grand village for almost a week as the tribe rested from its stressful ordeal. But, at the first opportunity, Tatarrax called a meeting of the Council of Chiefs. The chiefs of the three tribes closest to the Platte were in attendance when Tatarrax stood to address the collection of chiefs and sub-chiefs.

"Fellow Pawnee, we the Grands have just returned from a hunt into the hills to the north. During the trip back, we had a tragic confrontation with the Comanche in which there were heavy losses on both sides. I have called you together because I believe that the Comanche will not forget the loss of a chief and many braves to the Pawnee. However, I believe before too long they will attack us again in vengeance and we must be prepared to resist them. The three tribes represented here will, of course, be the most vulnerable to their attacks. I feel that all of us should strengthen our battle groups and we should work at giving these groups the training they will need to meet the onslaught of these powerful marauders."

None of the other chiefs objected to the words of Tatarrax and when a vote was taken, it was unanimous that action had to be taken to strengthen the fighting forces of the tribe. When the meeting adjourned, all of the leaders returned home vowing to correct the laxity that existed in the warrior groups of their respective people.

In the weeks that followed, workers were kept busy building defensive breastworks at various points around the Pawnee villages and every morning, the warriors of the various tribes could be seen practicing offensive and defensive tactics in the open fields around the villages. It wasn't long before the war-chiefs of the Pawnee had honed their fighting men to a fine cutting edge, a sight that would have placed fear into the hearts of any enemies of the Pawnee. Part of the reason for this was the outward appearance of the Pawnee braves. Their muscular physiques, their grim, somber facial expressions coupled with their shaven heads and scalp-locks all tended to make them a fearful lot.

*   *   *

At a massive village on the Dismal River, a large contingent of Comanche tried to heal their pride as they licked their wounds following their last contact with the Pawnee in buffalo country. Almost all of the braves that had fought the Pawnee had suffered some sort of injury. That, plus the loss of some twenty warriors including the Comanche chief, was a hard fact to swallow.

Once Palomona, the top chief of the Comanche, had fully realized what his tribe had suffered, he could think of nothing but revenge. This was definitely in the basic nature of the Comanche who were not accustomed to losing in the practice of warfare.

Palomona cursed the fact that the Skidi had pulled back to the Platte, because he certainly would have ordered his warriors to gain revenge against this smaller stock of Pawnee. He realized, however, that an attack on the villages of the Grand or the Tappage would require a great deal of preparation and the best fighters the Comanche could muster. As difficult as the undertaking seemed to Palomona, he still intended to carry it out at some time and at a place advantageous to the Comanche.

*   *   *

Essentially after adopting the earth lodge, the Pawnee lived more securely and warmly and they ate very well. The good life they were experiencing early in the spring of 1543 had lulled them into almost forgetting about the Comanche threat. Such was the situation in the village of the Grands at this point in time. Reality was not made manifest until one bright and cool day when two bronze and muscular scouts raced into the Grand settlement shouting an alarming message. Scurrying immediately to the lodge of Tatarrax, they reported that a very large contingent of Comanche was camped only about six miles directly to the north.

Tatarrax acted instantly. He gave orders to one of the heralds to ride to the Skidi village and warn them of the impending danger. He also instructed the other scout to alert the war-chiefs of the village and have the warrior forces man the various defenses that had been built for this very purpose.

Hurriedly, Tatarrax secured his weapons which consisted of a stumpy bow and quiver of arrows as well as a sharp iron axe and a steel sword that he had obtained from the Spanish conquistadores. As Tatarrax made his appearance at the head of his war-chiefs in front of the village breastworks, a loud cheer arose from the throng of grim-looking Pawnee braves who gained confidence and pride when last Tatarrax had lead them in a fight with the Comanche.

The rest of the day was spent anticipating an attack that did not come. Tatarrax then assumed that the attack would probably come the next day and he instructed his chiefs to have their men sleep in the defenses and that a sharp vigil be kept at all stations all night long. Like any other Pawnee brave, Tatarrax slept on the ground within one of the series of earthworks behind which the men of the Platte would defend the village.

*   *   *

As the sun rose the next day six miles north of the Platte River, several hundred Comanche warriors rose from their make-shift beds. Some broke their fast by eating buffalo jerk while others checked their weapons or applied war paint to their faces. Before too long, a lone drummer sat at the edge of a large flat area and began beating out the cadence for the Comanche War Dance. One by one, the Comanche braves began joining in the dance until mostly all were involved. War yelps filled the cool morning air as the fighters shuffled their feet and waved an assortment of weapons in the rhythmic beat. It was a frightful sight as the Padouca worked themselves into a warring frenzy.

After an hour of readying themselves emotionally, the Comanche bunched together in the middle of the flat clearing. Then, in a solid crescendo, the warriors burst forth from their huddle and raced across the prairie behind their war chief Palomona toward the settlement of the Grand Pawnee.

In the Pawnee defenses, the warriors of the Platte readied themselves for the attack that they knew was bound to come. Everything was quiet at mid-morning as the Pawnee scanned the hills to the north. The old veterans appeared to show no fear, but the young braves, who had not seen action before, fidgeted in their positions in the breastworks.

Suddenly, like the breaking of a thunderstorm, four hundred Comanche appeared on the hill tops overlooking the Pawnee village on the north. Palomona muscled his way through his eager braves and he studied the network of Pawnee defenses surrounding the encampment. Realizing he had lost the element of surprise, he was forced to call on Comanche pride to carry the fight to the

Pawnee. Raising a sturdy stone axe above his head with a bronze, muscular arm, he shouted: "These are the scavengers of the soil who are our enemies. Drive them from our land and from our river." Then, with one forward motion of his axe, the Comanche battle group poured down the slope and threw themselves at the tough knot of Pawnee. The clash of weapons was deafening as the attacking Comanche tried to climb into the breastworks to overcome the disadvantage at which they found themselves. Despite the aggressiveness of the sandhill marauders, the well-conditioned Pawnee held their own in the first assault, forcing their attackers to withdraw and regroup.

The failure of the initial strike against the defenses proved very frustrating to Palomona, who with the help of his lieutenants, hurried to reorganize the scattered fighters into an effective attacking force. Once this was accomplished, the determined Comanche slammed against the earthworks a second time. Death screams could be heard here and there along the network of defenses as weapons on both sides found their marks. Soon both sides of the earthworks were marked with bodies and blood.

Tatarrax exemplified Pawnee pride as he stood at a prominent position in the defenses wielding his Spanish sword, a weapon completely foreign to the Comanche and which scored heavily on the blitzing enemy. The chief never wavered and his strength seemed to grow as the melee continued. Because of the Pawnee leader's example, the defenders stiffened even more and eventually it was evident that the tide of battle was turning in favor of the Platte warriors. Shortly thereafter, most of the attacking Comanche realized that they were not going to crack the hard shell of the Grand village and for a second time, they began to fall back through their own dead. Once Palomona, who had survived the struggle, realized that his cause was lost, he called for a withdrawal from the bloody earthworks. Before too long, the vanquished Comanche retreated to the hills overlooking the Grand village. There the subdued force paused, took one last look at the tough defenses below and then departed into the vastness of the sandhills, the undisputed refuge of the Comanche.

CHAPTER IX

QUIVIRA REVISITED

The Pawnee Nation prospered and grew very strong under the guidance of the famed Tatarrax during the 1500's. In this time period, Spanish influence spread into the areas of today's Arizona and New Mexico. Among the Spaniards there, many believed that the cities of gold still existed somewhere on the sprawling wasteland to the north, but always the haunting thought of the ignominy of the Coronado expedition discouraged the authorities from conducting efforts in that direction.

Although Spain claimed the land of the Pawnee as part of its empire, only time could ease the bad memories engendered by the name "Quivira." Only time could instill an interest in elusive wealth that tempted men to gamble their very lives to find the land of riches where the very streets were paved with gold. It took almost sixty years for the conquerors of Mexico to heal their wounds and to garner enough spirit and lust to again penetrate the mysterious emptiness that was Quivira.

To curiously probe the obscure lies within the basic nature of man, hence it should not have been too surprising to the people of the Platte to once again observe the Spaniards in their role of the insatiable quest for gold.

The city of Santa Fe, New Mexico was founded by the Spaniards on the ruins of an old Indian settlement toward the end of the sixteenth century. About that time, the viceroy of New Spain appointed conquistador Juan de Onate as the governor of New Mexico. As was the case with most states in New Spain after the time of Cortes, New Mexico was in dire need of the wealth required for the proper development and government of the area.

Being one of those among the Spaniards who believed firmly that the golden cities existed somewhere on the great desert to the north and east of New Mexico, Onate, shortly after his appointment, made plans to form a fighting force and take it into the vast land first visited by Francisco Coronado. In this endeavor, he hoped to uncover the secret of the reputed "Mines of Quivira," since Spain claimed the area, and place them under his control. In forming his entrada (expedition), he chose fifty well armed and mounted soldiers as a nucleus. Around this core, he added about one hundred Indian warriors and some fifty Indian helpers who administered to the soldiers, braves, and animals.

Immediately under Onate's command was a young Spanish professional soldier, Captain Francisco Saldivar. Saldivar personified the true conquistador with his devotion to his profession and his stiff military bearing. He was also well reputed for being a very strict disciplinarian. It has been said that many soldiers had been executed and many Indians had been hanged by Saldivar for acts he considered to be traitorous to the Crown. With Saldivar in charge of his forces, Onate had little to worry about as far as his fighting men were concerned and this allowed him time to concentrate on the plans of the entrada.

THE CONQUEROR

Spanish-bred, ruthless and bold;

the king's envoy to explore.

In brilliant armor seeking gold,

he was the dreaded conquistador.

Onate was a great scholar of the Spanish conquests in the New World. He had "The Journal," the bible for all Spanish exploring expeditions, totally memorized and he had read every word written by Coronado during and after his ill-fated probe into Quivira. With the knowledge obtained from his studies, he was able to plot a direct course to Quivira and not wander endlessly as did the Coronado troop in New Mexico and Texas.

Once organized and equipped in the year 1599, the Onate force pushed northeast from Santa Fe and before long crossed the Canadian River into Oklahoma and Kansas. None of the soldiers or Indians on Onate's expedition had ever visited Quivira. The weapons and armor carried by the Onate force were not too much different from those of the Coronado army.

The early summer days were very hot and humid as the Onate brigade trudged across the flat, grassy Kansas plain. Once it had reached the Arkansas River, the soldiers were in a sorry state of exhaustion. At this point, Saldivar called a halt to the advancement of the column and ordered his men to rest, bathe, and restore their strength. This, the men greatly appreciated and they spent several days basking in the warm sun and relaxing in the cool water of the beautiful river.

Even though the Wichita Indians were prominent along the Arkansas at the time of the Onate probe, no village was observed by the Spaniards at the point where they reached the stream. However, one day during the expedition's recess when all parties were most relaxed, a party of Wichita warriors suddenly appeared near the Spanish camp. Some of the eight braves carried bows with quivers of arrows strapped to their backs. Others carried long sharp lances and all of the grim-looking fighters brandished sharp stone axes in their belts.

As the Wichita party viewed the Onate expedition, they appeared to show no fear. With the Spaniards looking on curiously, the Wichita moved toward the relaxing battle group. The Europeans realized that the small war party did not pose any threat, yet they wondered why they approached their camp. When the Wichita had moved in closer, their leader, wearing a magnificent buffalo cap, made gestures indicating his desire to see the head man of the expedition. Once summoned, Onate moved to face the haughty Wichita. Viewing the muscular Wichita with whom he had to speak, Onate called for Vojar, chief of his Indian contingent who might be able to communicate with the Wichita.

It was a highly interesting moment when Vojar confronted the Wichita leader. In order to find a common ground on which to communicate, Vojar began using words from the languages of tribes with which he had been in contact. Immediately upon using words from the Caddoan stock, the Wichita brightened up his sober mood and began attempting a full conversation with the Pueblo. Realizing that he could make some sense with the Wichita through gestures and Caddoan words, Vojar politely urged the Wichita to sit in a comfortable area and he invited Onate to join in the discourse.

Using every technique at his disposal to speak with the guest, it wasn't long before Vojar realized that the Wichita wanted the Spanish general to visit a large village and an important chief some miles to the west along the Arkansas. When Onate agreed to such a visit, the Wichita moved hurriedly to where he had left his comrades, and in a flash the warriors disappeared to carry the news to their home village.

Onate was happy for the contact with the Wichita because he felt that he could obtain some valuable information concerning Quivira and possibly the location of its mines of gold.

The day that Onate made the trip to the Wichita village, he was accompanied by only Saldivar, Vojar and five Indian warriors. This, he felt, would not make his host uneasy. As the Onate group approached the settlement, they could tell that it was possibly one of the major Wichita villages along the Arkansas. It consisted of several large earth lodges, a huge number of skin lodges and several bark huts. It could be seen that the inhabitants were well fed as almost every home had buffalo or deer meat drying in the sun near its entry way.

Very little attention was given the party by the villagers as it entered the encampment. Led by Vojar, who understood proper Indian protocol, the group moved toward the enclave of the village chief, who lived in a very large earth lodge beside which stood a tall lodge pole. From this pole hung several symbols of the chief's office plus some scalps taken in battle.

Vojar proceeded to the entrance of the lodge and there he began chanting a strange song of greeting. Almost as if he understood Vojar's message, a tall, distinguished Wichita with a highly decorated scalp-lock presented himself at the entrance to the dwelling. Here he greeted Vojar with his hand raised.

"I am Moscotol, chief of the western Wichita and I welcome you to our lands," spoke the dignified leader.

"Great leader, I want to present General Onate to you. He is the leader of our expedition and has stated that he is honored to be here," spoke Vojar. Following the introduction, the two leaders clasped hands and then Moscotol invited Onate, Vojar and Saldivar into his lodge. Here several women passed food and an excellent drink to the guests.

In the course of the conversation that followed, Moscotol indicated to the general that he would like the Wichita to become part of the Spanish Empire as he understood the Pawnee to be. On this, Onate understood why the Wichita chief was anxious to speak to him and this delighted him greatly because it offered the Spaniards the opportunity to befriend the Wichita Nation.

Responding to Moscotol's wish, Onate stood and in a ceremonious manner uttered these words: "As general of the Spanish forces in this area, I hereby declare that the western Wichita are, from this time forward, part of the Spanish Empire and subject to the Spanish Crown. In this regard, they are entitled to all of the privileges of the Spanish Empire."

Following these words, Onate embraced Moscotol and then presented him with a Spanish sword as a symbol of the joining of the two peoples. Moscotol became ecstatic and did a slow dignified dance on the lodge floor in order to express his joy.

Once the excitement of the ceremony had faded, Onate sought to gain some key information from the Wichita chief. "What can you tell me about the Pawnee that would be of help to us as we proceed to the Platte?" asked the general.

"The Pawnee are not very different from the Wichita," explained Moscotol, "You know the Pawnee and the Wichita had the same beginning and are of the same linguistic stock. The Pawnee tribes are very close and they are very fierce fighters. We have not had too much contact with them, so I do not know how they will receive white men today. That is all I can tell you."

"Do you know where they obtain the yellow metal that many people claim they have seen in their territory?" queried the conquistador.

"We have also heard stories of the yellow metal in Quivira, but we, the Wichita, have never seen such a metal, only the metal of which this sword is made," answered Moscotol.

"Do you think the metal exists in the Pawnee village?" asked Onate.

"I would not lie to a fellow citizen of the Spanish Empire," noted Moscotol, "but we Wichita do not believe that there is any of this desired metal in all the lands of Quivira."

Despite the words of the Wichita leader, who was one that should know about the existence of gold, Onate bade the chief and his tribe farewell, returned to camp, and made plans to proceed to the north and the villages of the people along the Rio de Jesus Maria (Platte).

Once leaving the Arkansas River, the Spanish army continued the long, hot trek to the northeast across the flat, haunting grasslands of northern Kansas. Even though anxious to contact the Pawnee, the Onate party did not meet with the Republican Pawnee when they crossed the Republican River in southern Nebraska.

The pace of the expedition was slowed by the Indian contingent that moved on foot, but on and on marched the men of Spain in what seemed an endless stretch of moor that never seemed to change. Suddenly, one day the flat prairie ended abruptly and the conquistadores found themselves overlooking a massive earth lodge village on the Platte. They had located the historic settlement of the Grand Pawnee that had occupied so much of Onate's thoughts in the months before. Once immediately across the river from the village, Onate called his forces to a halt because he was uncertain as to how to approach the mysterious Pawnee.

In the Grand Village, the head of the Council of Chiefs was Palati, the first son of Tatarrax and Pariki. Palati had earlier been made aware of the presence of the force of white men across the river and had made preparations to meet them with a force of about four hundred armed warriors.

Across the river, Onate called Vojar and Saldivar to his side. The trio at once began discussing what their next step might be in introducing themselves to the chief of the largest populace on the Platte. With their relatively small brigade, they obviously could not assault the settlement and it was Onate's wish that they contact the Pawnee in a manner in which they would approach any branch of the Spanish Empire.

As the trio debated about their approach and the rest of the soldiers and Indians cooled off in the waters of the river, the problem concerning the Pawnee was suddenly solved as Palati and four hundred bare-chested braves made their appearance on the opposite side of the wide stream. Palati and about half of his men were mounted on Spanish horses and the other half stood on foot carrying long sharp lances and highly decorated shields. Several drummers beat out a cadence on skin drums as the braves on foot stomped their feet and clapped their lances against their shields in time with the drums. This, of course, created a frightening sound and added to the feeling of the moment.

Without delay, Onate, Vojar and Saldivar mounted their steeds and leaving the rest of the brigade behind, they proceeded across the shallow water to meet the Pawnee at water's edge.

With his right hand raised in a symbol of peace, Vojar, the Pueblo, called out with words that he felt the Pawnee chief might comprehend and appreciate: "We have come here in peace and sincerely wish to become friends with the great Pawnee Nation."

Palati seeing that the trio was of no great threat, answered Vojar's words: "We can see that you mean us no harm. Come ashore so that we can hold council here on the cool bank of the river."

As the trio left the river, they dismounted, tied their horses to trees on the bank, and then took seats on some large logs half-buried in the sand along the shore. Palati dismounted in turn and took a seat on the sand near the visitors. He was the first to speak and Vojar did his best to pass the message along to Onate and Salvidar.

"We know who you are and for years we have wondered when the Spaniards would return to the land of the Pawnee. A long time ago when my father, Tatarrax, was chief of this land, the great general Coronado adopted us into the Empire of Spain. You see, I still hold my father's sword given him by the Spanish general. You also see our horses, descendants of those given us by Coronado.

"We, the Pawnee, welcome you and you are free to camp here along the great river. My braves will soon bring fresh food from our supplies and also, you have my permission to hunt for food in the area."

Onate and Salvidar were greatly taken with Palati. Indeed, Tatarrax must have been a great man to have raised such a son here in the wilderness and indeed, Coronado must have used great judgement in proclaiming these Pawnee as members of the Spanish Empire, they thought.

"Thank you for your kind generosity," said Onate to the Pawnee chief. "We are very happy that you are our brothers within our great empire. We will accept your kind offer of food for we are in dire need of sustenance. We will make our camp across the river and try not to disrupt your village. If you need any help from us of any kind, just let us know. Again, I thank you and I should like to speak to you again in a few days."

Following Onate's words, the Spaniard clasped Palati's hand and then mounted his colorful steed and recrossed the river followed by his two comrades. As he rode, Juan de Onate couldn't help but compare in his mind the vast difference between the Spanish conquest of Mexico and the annexation of the Pawnee and Wichita Nations.

Chapter X

Savage Star

Life was peaceful in the Onate camp for several days as the brigade bathed, rested and regained its strength on food obtained along the river and from the generous Pawnee. One bright, cool morning, however, the peace was broken as two Pawnee braves rode their ponies at full speed across the shallow waters of the Platte. Quickly alerted, Onate and his Indian interpreter ran to meet them.

"We have just received word that our enemy, the Comanche, are approaching our village with a large war party," said one of the braves. "Palati has asked if you with your army will help us defend our village?"

Quickly, many thoughts crossed Onate's mind. He could refuse and no one would blame him, yet this would be an excellent opportunity to seal his pact with Palati and show the Spanish concern for their fellow subjects of the Crown.

"Tell Palati that I will ready my soldiers and Indian warriors and we will meet him on the north side of the village,"
shouted Onate. Hearing the interpretation of the general's
words from Vojar, the Pawnee raced across the river to
carry the word to their chief.

It wasn't long before fifty mounted conquistadores in
steel helmets and iron breast plates followed Onate across
the river followed by one hundred armed Indian warriors.
Both contingents of this army carried the dreaded, traditional Spanish spears and pikes as well as well-tempered
swords and daggers. Responding to the orders of the
famed Captain Saldivar, they were indeed an awesome
looking group.

Once across the Platte, Onate led his troop along the
east side of the massive settlement until reaching the
northern edge. When turning to the west, the general
observed Palati in front of about a thousand braves on foot
each armed with a bow and arrows. Off to the west stood
about one hundred more warriors mounted on ponies and
armed with spears and the famed Pawnee war clubs.

As Saldivar arranged his troops alongside the Pawnee, a
loud cheer arose from the ranks of the fierce force of
braves. Once in position, the Spaniards awaited the
orders of Palati who would pick the ground where they
would meet the Comanche. The hearts of the younger
Spanish soldiers stuck in their throats as they anticipated
the battle, for they had never met in battle with any fighters of the likes of the reputed Comanche.

With one forward motion of his war club, Palati ordered
the huge army to move in a northerly direction. Upon
moving about a league, the composite of fighters reached
a ridge which overlooked a large valley to the north from

which Palati expected the Comanche to emerge. Here the force halted and waited.

As Palati, Onate, and Saldivar consulted, it wasn't long before an approaching column of Comanche came into view. To Onate, it appeared that the Comanche were out manned by the composite battle group that awaited them. This sent questions through Onate's mind about the Comanche. "Were they such great fighters that numbers didn't count? Was their pride greater than their intelligence?" he asked himself.

Onate's questions were soon answered as the Comanche chief, in full war bonnet, halted his braves in full view of the Pawnee and their allies perched on the ridge above him. Viewing the armored Spanish soldiers, he realized that something was not quite right in the Pawnee war party. Who were these strangers dressed in metal shirts with their odd looking lances raised against the sky?

Almost immediately, something told the Comanche leader that he had better not test the sinister wall of steel helmets and breast plates that blocked his way and he could hear the panic in the conversation among his men. In a manner so unaccustomed of the Comanche, the brightly dressed chief, who no doubt anticipated a great victory, ordered his fighting men around and before long, they disappeared into the sandhills whence they came.

What a moral victory for Palati! He had accomplished something that no other leader of the Pawnee had ever accomplished. He had turned back a bristling force of fierce Comanche without so much as firing an arrow in their direction. In this feat, he knew he owed Onate and his men a great deal of credit. In order to show his gratitude, he ordered a celebration in the village to honor the Spaniards and their Indian contingent.

The Pawnee, who were usually very grim and solemn, broke out their best food and drink. They danced by open fire and feasted late into the night in tribute to their European and Indian brethren. The visitors from the southwest were not of the kind to turn down praise and favors and they heartily joined with the Pawnee in reveling in their mutual "victory."

As the sun rose on the Platte valley and the Grand village the next day, everything was in disarray. Weapons and equipment were scattered everywhere and soldiers and warriors slept where they had dropped from the weariness of celebration. Only Palati, Onate and Saldivar had restrained themselves enough to find shelter within the chief's earth lodge.

It took most of the new day for the celebrants to nurse themselves back to normalcy and to recover their horses and belongings. Luckily for the Pawnee village and the Spanish force, the Comanche had not changed their minds in their retreat away from the Grand settlement.

After several days, when conditions had settled down in the Spanish camp following the Comanche incident, Onate felt that the time was right for a serious discussion with the Pawnee chief concerning the presence of gold in Quivira. Very early one morning, Onate crossed the river on his steed and entered the village to seek out Palati. To Onate's surprise, he observed much activity in the village despite the early hour. As the general approached the center of the earth lodges, he observed a sight that nearly knocked him from his horse. In the middle of the ceremonial grounds, the Pawnee had erected a scaffold and it was completely surrounded by the residents of the village. On the framework of the scaffold, Onate observed a young girl in a painted buffalo robe bound spreadeagle on the framework. Facing east, the left side of her body was painted black and the right side, red.

What Onate did not realize was that he was witnessing the ceremony of the Captive Girl Sacrifice of the Pawnee. The sacrifice was a rite dedicated to the Morning Star to ensure a bountiful harvest of the planted crops. Capturing a teenaged girl from an enemy camp, the Pawnee would first treat her with great kindness, giving her the finest in food and dress. On the peak day of the Morning Star ceremony, she was dressed in a buffalo robe and her body painted black (to signify night) and red (to signify day). Before daybreak, she was brought to the scaffold and bound. The tribe would gather about the scaffold, smoke, chant and sing as the priests of the tribe would climb the scaffold. Then as the first rays of sun light would appear over the horizon, a brave would step forward and shoot an arrow into the girl's heart. Another brave would make an incision above her heart with a knife and he would then daub his face and body with her blood and allow some of her blood to drip onto buffalo meat laid beneath the scaffold. Four braves would then carry the body about a quarter of a mile to the east of the village where they would leave her to the scavengers and the elements. The ceremony would close with the participants eating the buffalo meat as the tribe danced, sang and participated in unrestrained sexual activities, all in tribute to the Morning Star.

Visualizing the bound girl, Onate immediately realized that she was to fall victim to some pagan ritual. This

turned his stomach even though as a Spanish conquistador, he was fully accustomed to seeing bloodshed. Some
things became clear to Onate as he looked on at the ceremony. He realized that the maiden was no doubt a
Comanche captive and this was probably the reason the
Comanche had initially decided to attack the Pawnee.

Without any concern for himself, Onate ran through the
gathered crowd, ascended the scaffold and with his dag-
ger, cut the girl loose. Then drawing his sword, he chal-
lenged the priests and armed braves on the platform.
Instead of attacking Onate, the participants looked upon
him with awe. This man must command some powerful
spiritual medicine to interfere in a ritual to the Morning
Star, they thought.

As Onate stood by the girl with his sword drawn, Palati
climbed the ladder to the top of the scaffold. Immediately,
Onate began lecturing him. "What kind of pagans are you
that you will kill a girl for the sake of some foolish ritual?"
he asked. Are these the brave Pawnee who hunt the buffalo or fight the undaunted Comanche? This is behavior
unbecoming of subjects of the Spanish Crown and I want
her returned to her people immediately!"

Palati wanted no trouble with Onate, so he stood facing
his people giving them the signal to abandon the rite.
Slowly the Pawnee and the participants withdrew from the
area in a disgruntled mood.

"The ceremony dedicated to the Morning Star is an old
religious rite practiced by the Pawnee long before my
father and grandfather led our people," said Palati.

"You really don't believe that this murder helps your
people?" asked Onate.

"We believe that it helps because as far back as our spoken history takes us, we have always had good crops of the maize. However, I will consider your wise words in deciding whether we will continue the practice. Also, I will consult with your friars as to whether they believe the great Tirawa looks with favor on this kind of ceremony. I will have the women of the tribe clean up the girl and we will return her to her people. Maybe it will help to improve our relations with the Comanche."

Onate believed Palati's words and they helped him relax as he walked with the chief to his lodge. "I came here today to speak to you on some very important matters, but because of my experience today, I am exhausted. I will return to my camp and be back another day to speak on these matters that are essential to the Crown of Spain."

Palati fully understood Onate's feelings and he walked with the general to where his horse was tied. Onate then moved across the river still in shock by the age-old practice of the peaceful people of the Platte.

CHAPTER XI

BLOOD ON THE SUN

One night as Palati, the son of Tatarrax, sat in his lodge, he dwelt on the incident surrounding the ceremony of the Morning Star. As he thought of the Comanche girl and Onate's reaction to the rite, he had mixed feelings. In one way, he could understand Onate's actions because he knew that the white man placed great value on human life and he realized that he had great respect for women. This, of course, was quite different from the Pawnee who mostly considered women as a commodity, who were something to be bargained for and who only played secondary roles in the affairs of the tribe.

On the other hand, Palati resented Onate interfering in a Pawnee affair. The Pawnee were Spanish citizens, but Onate was not a Pawnee chief and he had not earned the right to exercise any authority in the people's encampment. Onate wanted to speak with Palati about matters of great importance, but Palati felt also that he should speak to the general about an important matter...how to gain respect within the Pawnee Nation. Thus he vowed that he would visit Onate at the first opportunity.

Following two sleeps, Palati rode a beautiful Spanish barb across the Platte at an early morning hour and entered the quiet Spanish camp. Riding up to the general's tent, he was warmly greeted by the leader who was seated outside enjoying the cool morning air.

"I am happy to have you visit us, Palati," said the general, "but something must be weighing on your mind."

"Yes," answered the chief. "I have been thinking about the ceremony the other day. It is my feeling that even though we the Pawnee are Spanish subjects, you had no authority to interrupt a ritual that has been a Pawnee tradition for a hundred years."

Onate did not want to offend the Pawnee because he felt he would need his help and advice at a later time, so he sought to appease the disturbed chief. "I am sorry about what happened, but the near sacrifice of the young, innocent girl shocked me deeply. I thought you understood my feelings. What can I do now to restore my image among your people?"

"There is one thing that you can do to gain some authority and great respect among the Grands, and that would be to participate in the Sun Dance and submit to the rite called Okipa," explained Palati.

Palati's words captured the total attention of Onate and completely whet his curiosity. "Why does the Sun Dance command so much respect from the Pawnee?" asked the general.

Palati hesitated for a moment. He did not know how to answer Onate's question, but then he knew he better be truthful. "It is a ritual that is extemely painful and strongly tests the strength of the subject. Some braves refuse to go through it and some do not hold up under it. If a brave survives this rite, however, he is regarded as a hero by the entire tribe for all time."

Onate thought about the challenge he personally was receiving from the Pawnee chief. He thought about the pride of the Spanish Empire and the pride of the Spanish conquistadores who he represented. "Have you gone through this torture?" Onate asked Palati.

"Yes, here are the scars," answered Palati as he pointed to the long marks on each side of his chest.

"You leave me no choice," grunted Onate, "since true Spanish soldiers do not back down from challenges of this kind. Let me know when you want me to come to the village for the rite."

"I will go now and make preparations for your entry into the Sun Dance ceremony," said Palati. "When we are ready, I will come to let you know, but you must come of your own willingness." On those words, the Pawnee leader mounted his barb and rode proudly across the river.

With the Pawnee, any ceremony that had to do with the raising of corn or the hunting of buffalo carried a religious connotation because of the importance of the gathering of food for the tribe. Hence, many times the Sun Dance was combined with the ceremony of the Dance of the Maize or the ceremony of the Buffalo Dance to add to its significance. In preparing for the Sun Dance, which usually took place in mid-summer when the sun was in full brilliance, a Sun Lodge was erected and the tribe celebrated for three days by playing games, smoking, listening to speeches of thanksgiving for the receipt of corn or buffalo, dancing and praying.

The last day of the Sun Dance celebration featured the Okipa ceremony. This act, which was strictly a means of gaining hero status in the tribe, was voluntary and was entered into by many chiefs, warriors, and medicine men.

The act opened with the volunteers being rounded up by members of some military group such as the Buffalo Society. These volunteers were then bound, mocked, and led to the Sun Lodge. Here they had wooden skewers driven into the skin and muscles of the upper chest. In this act, the participants could not utter any sign of pain. If they did, they were eliminated from the ceremony.

Buckskin thongs were then tied to the skewers and thrown over the beams of the lodge supporting the roof. The buckskin was then used to lift the volunteer up in the air where he dangled and twisted in agony. The few white men who had been permitted to view this ceremony were utterly shocked by it claiming that it reminded them of a form of crucifixion. Even some Indians witnessing the act for the first time would slash themselves with knifes to express their deep sympathy for the subject of the ceremony.

Occasionally during the time course of the rite, the volunteer would be lowered so that he could rest. At these times, attending women would wipe the blood from the celebrant. When dangling on the buckskin, the volunteer was required to turn his face with eyes open into the blazing sun shining through a large hole in the roof of the Sun Lodge. If at any time the subject of the torture appeared to wince or shrink from the pain in his eyes, he would be disgraced for life. In the last phase of the ritual, the subject was lowered to the ground and upon mustering up his residual strength, he would pull and tear away at the skewers and buckskin thongs until his flesh and skin parted, freeing himself. At this point, the participant was administered to by the women at the ceremony. In this time, they were admired by the rest of the witnesses as distinguished heroes, which they truly were.

With the time approaching for the Sun Dance in the Grand village, Palati had accepted three Pawnee volunteers for Okipa. One was a young chieftain, one a warrior with the Buffalo Society, and the other a young applicant for entry into the Clan of Medicine Men. All of these Pawnee were much younger than Onate and Palati wondered how Onate would hold up. Deep in his heart, he hoped Onate would survive the rigors of the grueling test.

On the last day of the Sun Dance celebration in the village, Palati sent a courier to the Spanish camp to summon Onate. As the Spanish general prepared for the visit to the Indian encampment and as he rode his steed across the shallow Platte waters, many thoughts crossed his mind. "I am a Spanish general and yet here I am submitting to torture by savages," he thought. "I am used to handing out punishment, not receiving it. I don't really have to do this."

Like a true conquistador, the general put all fear and doubts behind him and rode unhesitatingly to assume his responsibility. Upon arriving at the lodge of Palati, he was welcomed into the lodge and there the Pawnee chief sought to indoctrinate him in the ordeal that he was to experience the next day. As Palati described the Okipa ritual, Onate tried to keep his composure, for this was the first time in his experience that he was to face personal injury without his helmet, steel shirt, and sword and the ability to fight back.

"The ceremony is going to be a strenuous and painful experience, so I suggest that you eat well today and get plenty of rest to face tomorrow. We have prepared plenty of delicious food and a comfortable bed for you. Take advantage of these things because in Okipa you will need all the strength you can muster," added Palati.

The rest of the day, Onate sat in the lodge contemplating the misery he would face and how he might bear up under this form of stress. He had experienced many wounds and deep pain in his years as a soldier, but would this be the same? The general ate the wonderful food and then he relaxed on his bed still in wonderment of the trial he would face on the new day.

In the morning of the next day, Onate was "captured" by members of the Pawnee Buffalo Society, the main military society of the tribe. With hands bound behind him, the Spanish general was led away toward the center of the village and into the very large earth lodge dedicated to the Sun. Led through the large crowd assembled within the structure, Onate was positioned at the center of the floor along with the other three captives who were also bound.

A drummer in the middle of the viewing crowd suddenly began beating out a slow but consistent cadence and soon the crowd chimed in with mocking chants, as if to say to the captives that they would collapse under the impending torture. Once the drumming and chanting stopped, all eyes fell on the members of the military group that moved from captive to captive, stripping off their shirts. The military group then began driving sharp wooden skewers into the skin and under the muscles of the chest near each armpit of each of the subjects. This was done in an extremely harsh way in order to create pain. Without doubt, the pain associated with positioning the skewers was an excruciating experience. However, none of the victims uttered a sound in the process, but the deep disturbance reflected on each face in a manner resembling a death mask.

Long buckskin thongs were then tied to the skewers and the other ends were thrown over the large beams supporting the roof of the lodge. Several members of the Buffalo Society then lifted each of the captives off the floor and left them hanging and churning in extreme misery. At first, Onate did not seem to feel the horrendous pain, but that was because he had momentarily fainted from the agonizing strain.

At this point in the ceremony, the crowd turned from mocking the victims to cheering in support. Once conscious, the bare-chested Spaniard realized that he was experiencing a throbbing, deep and unbearable torture. Not uttering a sound, Onate glanced at his fellow sufferers and he could see that he was holding up as well as they.

The victims received a temporary reprieve from their anguish after dangling for several minutes, when they were lowered to the ground. All four captives had trouble keeping their balance and standing once brought to the floor, but they were supported by several women who also wiped the blood from their chests, legs and feet. At this point, the members of the Buffalo Society instructed each of the participants to stare at the sun blazing through the large opening in the roof and to hold this stare while being elevated and while dangling a second time.

Up and up, the captives were lifted again as they turned their faces to the full brilliance of the celestial body. To Onate, this was double torture, yet all four celebrants remained silent. Only the writhing of their heads and bodies exposed the excruciating torment to the cheering crowd below. With his eyes wide open, Onate felt that he would completely lose his sight or suffer damage to his eyes from the radiance beaming down on the lodge. The general lost all track of time as he suffered through the multiple torture and he did not realize what was happening in the ceremony until his feet again touched the ground. Once more, he had to be supported in order to remain standing while the women wiped the blood from his chest.

The four participants next entered the final phase of the Okipa while receiving the loud chants of encouragement form the privileged audience in the Sun Lodge. In this phase, the loose ends of the buckskin thongs, still over the roof beams of the lodge, were anchored to the center supports of the structure. Following this, the four victims were instructed to strain at the buckskin and pull the wooden skewers loose form their chest muscles and skin. As they began this final step, Onate found this struggle against the thongs to be as painful as when he hung above the floor and even bloodier.

Anxious to end the agony, Onate tugged extremely hard at the skewers by digging his heels into the dirt floor. Suddenly, the left skewer ripped through his flesh and flew loose. Onate hadn't realized that the pain resulting would be so deep and excruciating. Glancing across the lodge, the Spaniard could see that each of the Pawnee victims had also struggled loose from one of their skewers and blood was everywhere on the floor.

Mustering up the last bit of energy in his body, Onate yanked at the second skewer in his chest. On a final stroke with convulsing torment, the right skewer pulled through the muscle on Onate's front and he fell to the floor. Blood streaked down his chest and soaked into the ground next to the exhausted celebrant. With this, the crowd roared their approval of the first one to finish the torturous initiation. Soon after, however, the three Pawnee finished their extremely punishing experience as well.

All four of those who had gone through the grueling activity remained on the floor as the Pawnee women administered to their needs, most serious of which was the stopping of the bleeding. In order to get the crowd worked up over the totally spent heroes, the drummer in the lodge began beating out a hurried cadence. Again the Pawnee crowd shook the rafters of the Sun Lodge with their cheers and yelps for their men of honor. As for Onate, the tribesmen now had thoroughly forgiven him for his interference in the Morning Star rite. He was now one of their own.

The Pawnee chief moved from hero to hero congratulating them. Finally he stopped to check on the man from Spain. He took extra pains looking after the conquistador and after some time, helped him to his feet and assisted him in the walk to his lodge where he could convalesce. When Palati and Onate had left the Sun Lodge, the crowd converged on the Pawnee "Sons of the Sun" to help them. When the crowd and their heroes had left the lodge, the celebration continued as the tribal members set fire to the structure and danced and chanted until it burned to the ground. In the eyes of the Pawnee, the total observance was a huge success, but to Onate the experience was one he would never forget and not want to repeat.

Completely exhausted and hurting, Onate moved to the bed prepared for him in the chief's lodge. In the eyes of Palati and his family, Onate was a hero of the first degree because they remembered too well when Palati had suffered through the Okipa rite after reaching chieftain rank. As a result of the Pawnee respect for heroes, Palati and his wife moved from the lodge to another dwelling close by leaving only their beautiful daughter, Totta, to administer to Onate's needs.

The general slept without stirring until noon of the next day. However, because he still felt tremendous pain in his chest and back, he remained in bed welcoming the efforts of Totta to feed him and make him comfortable. The Spaniard could not help but admire Totta's attributes as she moved about the lodge. He judged that she was in her twenties and probably the prettiest girl in the Pawnee village. She had an alluring smile and a very handsome, bronzed face capped by beautiful, long black hair that was drawn and tied to the side of her head. Through her light summer robe, Onate recognized that she had a very shapely figure that stirred Onate's manly desires even through the severe pain he felt. He could not help but wonder why Palati had left this lovely creature alone in the lodge with him. He figured that perhaps the chief felt that he was harmless with his wounds and pains, so he decided that he would refrain from touching the stunning girl.

As night fell on the Grand village again, Onate was quick to fall asleep in his very comfortable bed. In the darkest part of the night, the Spanish leader was awakened by a very unusual sensation, the touch of a soft, warm body next to his aching chest. Immediately, he recognized that his bed companion was Totta. At this point, Onate decided not to ask any questions about Indian customs as he surrounded the girl with his arms and kissed her passionately. This sent electric sensations of the painless variety through the soldier's whole body. Before much longer, the rugged conquistador totally lost all sense of pain as the sensations of pleasure completely took over his body. Undoubtedly, Totta, though young, recognized the right treatment for a body steeped in pain. As Onate held Totta close there in the darkness of the lodge, eventually complete exhaustion took over and the general fell into a deep sleep.

The sun was high in the sky on the next day as Onate woke to face Palati and his smiling daughter. The Pawnee chief appeared pleased that his Spanish friend was recovering well. Totta, as well, appeared extremely happy even though she understood that she could not keep the general from pursuing his assigned goals. Hence, when it was time for Onate to return to his men, she made no attempt to hold him.

CHAPTER XII

FOOL S GOLD

No one knows where the story originated that the villages of Quivira were paved with gold, but the success experienced in sacking the treasures of Mexico was no doubt the impetus that spurred on the soldiers of Spain to investigate the story. Up to the time of Onate, the Spaniards had spent huge sums of wealth, many lives, and great amounts of effort and time seeking out these villages without finding one small grain of the precious metal.

Once Onate had fully recovered from the consequences for the Sun Dance, he again decided to speak with Palati about the main subject on his mind. On a warm, humid day in early August, he rode uninhibited across the shallow Platte and into the Grand settlement. Again he met Palati at the chief's lodge and was openly invited into the friendly atmosphere within.

As the two leaders sat face to face, Onate approached the head Pawnee about the main objective of the Spanish expedition. "Palati, ever since the Spanish people have been aware of Quivira, they have heard stories of the fabulous amount of yellow metal in the area. We have come here looking for the yellow metal because it is very valuable in our world. To you and the Pawnee, however, it is worth nothing. I have come here today to tell you that the yellow metal makes our empire strong. As a subject of Spain, I know you would want to increase the power of the Crown. I have also come here to ask you if you might know where the mines of Quivira exist. You and I both would gain great favor with the Spanish king if we could find the mines and the cities where this metal is in great abundance."

Palati looked at Onate with disbelief and then remarked: "We Pawnee have no yellow metal. You have spent enough time among us to know that no gold exists here or in the other Pawnee tribes. In my whole life, I have not seen nor heard of any in this whole area known as Quivira.

"I do not know where the stories of the metal started, but our braves have wandered wide and far and never have they returned with word of gold. The only wealth the Pawnee have is our horses, maize and buffalo. I speak the truth about the Pawnee, but maybe you can find the riches you seek in the land of the Kansa south and east of here. That land is also spoken of as Quivira, but we have not had any contact with the people there."

"I know you speak the truth and I have no reason to doubt your word," said Onate. "You are a great chief of a great people and we are proud that you are subjects of the great Spanish Empire. Time is running out for us. We must be about our quest for gold and return to New Mexico before the cold winds begin to blow. Tomorrow we will leave and move to the land of the Kansa, as you suggest. So I want to bid you 'farewell' now. I hope you have a long life looking after your good family and your people."

On Onate's words, the two leaders clasped hands and then the dignified general climbed his steed and rode swiftly from the village never to return.

The next morning saw the Spanish caravan on the move again. This time they trekked in a southeasterly direction by-passing the Republican Pawnee, but following the valley of the Republican River to another facet of the fabelled Kingdom of Quivira and another experience in failure.

*   *   *

The Kansa tribe of the state of Kansas belongs to the large Siouan linguistic stock. The original habitat of this stock is not known, however, it is believed to have been located in the Appalachian mountains. When forced by the pressure of the white man, these people began a western migration which eventually reached the country of the Great Lakes. One group of this original stock, some time before 1540, appears to have moved down the Ohio River finally reaching the Mississippi River. Here the people separated with some persons moving downstream and some upstream. Those people who moved upstream known as the "Omaha" eventually reached the Des Moines River and they followed the river to its headwaters in Minnesota. From Minnesota, they wandered into North Dakota, South Dakota and Iowa eventually settling in a village at the juncture of the Big Sioux River and the Missouri River near the present-day Nebraska-South Dakota border. It was from this point that the Kansa broke off from the Omaha parent group because of a quarrel over wild game. Following this separation, the Kansa gens or Wind People moved down the Missouri and settled along a large tributary that now bears their name. Here, this branch of the Siouan stock prospered and built large villages of bark huts and tepees. With their prosperity, the various settlements of the Kansa became very strong supported by many powerful chiefs and experienced warriors.

*   *   *

One day, as the Spanish caravan moved down the Republican River, the forward scouts were suddenly confronted by a band of nine natives, some of whom were on foot and some mounted on Spanish mustangs similar to those in the caravan. The Indians showed no fear and remained in one position waiting for the mounted scouts to act. Since the sight of the Spanish steeds aroused curiosity among the scouts, they turned their mounts around and rode at full speed to report their find to Onate.

Hearing the report, Onate called for Vojar, the interpreter, to join him. Then accompanied by ten of his armored cavalrymen, he rode to talk to the Indian party who still remained at their original position. Vojar and Onate rode forward to speak to the brazen warriors and in doing so, Onate could tell that the sight of them totally confused Vojar. The interpreter addressed the warriors, who were armed with lances and long bows and arrows, with a salutary phrase in Caddoan, but it was obvious that they could not understand. One of the braves answered Vojar in the Siouan tongue, but the Pueblo could not grasp the message.

"These people are not Wichita or Pawnee and they speak a tongue that is difficult for me to grasp," said Vojar to his general. Onate instructed Vojar to try to make some sense out of what appeared to be gibberish to the Pueblo. After some time, using single words and gestures, Vojar finally understood the message the braves wanted to convey.

"They are of the Kansa tribe located some distance down this river," Vojar told Onate. "They said that they are a powerful people who have been in contact with white men before. They do not like whites because they have suffered at their hands. They say we are not welcome in their villages and want us to leave or face attacks from their people." Once the Kansa realized that Vojar and Onate understood their communication, they turned and proceeded down the river.

Despite the word that the Kansa were a powerful people, both Onate and Saldivar maintained their military arrogance. They did not feel that any primitive force could deter the caravan equipped with steel and leather armor, steel pikes, crossbows and a variety of swords and stilettos. They believed that the mere sight of the conquistadores donning the black helmets that completely covered their faces would be enough to compel most adversaries to turn and run. Hence, after camping overnight, the shaken but proud Onate ordered his army to continue its penetration down the Republican River.

Following three more days on the trail, the caravan arrived at the juncture of the Republican and Kansas Rivers. Along with the viewing of the joining of the two rivers, Saldivar and Onate became aware of two different large encampments along the Kansas. One camp appeared to be a permanent settlement made up mostly of bark homes. The other consisted purely of colorful tepees. Almost as soon as viewing the two camps, the Spanish leaders became aware of two huge warrior forces that were present on their left side and left flank. It was also immediately evident to the Spaniards that they were trapped between the rivers and the massive war-parties.

The sight was a humbling one for Onate and his men. It did not take a Spanish general to realize that the caravan was far outnumbered and if a fight began, the Spaniards and their Indian allies would soon be overwhelmed despite their armament. The Spanish lust for the yellow metal soon changed to thoughts of survival, so without hesitation Onate called his column to a halt.

Studying the two forces that had them surrounded, it was obvious to Onate that two different tribes were involved. One tribe dressed like the scouts he had spoken with, but the other people wore peculiar robes and many donned unusual fur caps not seen before by the Spaniards.

It was not long before the leaders of the two Indian forces joined each other and rode forward to speak with Onate and Vojar at the head of the Spanish column. Hoping that he would be understood, Vojar used the Caddoan tongue that he had learned among the Wichita and the Pawnee to utter some friendly terms. This appeared to be understood by the chief in the odd looking cap. In somewhat imperfect Caddoan, the chief did not hesitate to issue what was on his mind.

"You have invaded the territory of the Kansa people who live along this river. The chief with me is Thugina, their leader. I am Ekte, chief of these Osage warriors who are cousins of the Kansa."

"We are not your enemy and have come in peace," offered Vojar.

"The Kansa have seen other white men in the past and they also said that they were peaceful," said Ekto, "but later, they hanged many Kansa for not finding them the yellow metal."

Upon relaying Ekte's words to Onate, Vojar and the general held a brief conference after which Vojar continued his exchange with the Osage chief.

"What was the name of the leader of the white men of whom you speak?" queried Vojar.

"The Kansa did not learn anything about those people nor did they learn the leader's name," answered Ekte. "They were not here long, but in that time they killed many. We are not a warring people, but we do not trust the white man and we will not allow you into the villages. You can camp tonight up the river, but you must leave in the morning or we will attack and defeat your army."

Even though Onate did not totally understand the Osage chief, he could tell that he was serious. Because of the superiority of the Kansa and Osage forces, Onate did not want to antagonize them. Hence, he instructed Vojar to tell Ekte that he would comply.

On orders from Captain Saldivar, the Spanish army did an about-face and moved upriver for about one mile and set up camp for the night.

That night as Onate rested in his tent, he was stunned and confused. He could not believe the words of the Osage chief and the fact that the Kansa were riding Spanish horses. If another Spanish expedition had been exploring here, why was he not informed of it? Who was the Spanish general who led such an expedition? These logical questions caused a feeling of great despair to permeate through Onate's already tired consciousness. He felt totally betrayed.

At sunrise of the next day, the Onate expedition found itself on the trail again, only this time in retreat toward New Mexico and home for most of the Spanish soldiers. Like so many Spanish expeditions before it, the Onate probe had failed to extract a grain of gold from the great American desert. This, despite the expenditure of a great fortune in the undertaking. The Onate probe was not the first, and would not be the last, to gamble so much in the hapless quest of the gold of fools.

Chapter XIII

Terminus

Despite the expeditionary failures that the Spaniards had suffered in the search for the gold of the Kingdom of Quivira, it is incredible that in the final analysis they continued this effort off and on over the period of one hundred and eighty years. Immediately following the typically fruitless probe of Onate, Spain suspended her interest in Quivira becoming more involved in her hold on New Mexico.

Regardless of the Spanish disinterest in the areas about Quivira, the French began advancing their attention westward and southward out of Canada and, even more importantly, northward from the French possession of Louisiana. Curiously, by the middle of the seventeenth century, French trappers and fur traders were well entrenched with the Indian tribes along the drainage of the Missouri River and some of its tributaries. Usually traveling in pairs, some of these adventurers came by canoe moving from one waterway to another while others came by horse leading a packhorse laden with supplies or items of barter. These opportunists sometimes called "mountain men" dressed in buckskin with coats made of heavy blanket material or buffalo hide. Their feet were usually covered with buckskin leggings and either fur hats or stocking caps donned their hairy heads.

For protection, these trapper-traders carried long knives, hatchets, and flintlock rifles with extremely long barrels. Also among their possessions, these Frenchmen carried powder horns, bullet molds, lead, and several beaver traps. Their main objective was the securing of the prized beaver pelt needed for the stylish "beaver hat" in the markets of the East and Europe. The trappers took great risks to obtain beaver as they operated in the waters claimed by many fierce Indian tribes. Some of the tribes looked with disdain upon the fur traders while other tribes welcomed them with the realization that they were the only source of items from the eastern markets.

Once the French trappers had obtained a good number of beaver pelts, they faced the huge task of getting them to market. They usually flattened the pelts into one hundred pound bales and transported them in this form to the nearest trading post. The traders equipped with horses had a fairly easy task in this regard, but those with only canoes found themselves portaging both canoe and bales to get their prize to market.

When in civilized areas, these men of the frontier were known as the loudest, toughest, crudest men alive. In reality, civilization owes these men very much because they were the breed of men who first broke the trails and acquired the knowledge of the conditions and people in a very rugged land, which would prove to be of great advantage to those who followed.

In the connection established with the Indians, many French missionaries of the likes of Marquette, Hennepin, and the LaSalles began to spread their influences among the tribes of the Great Plains. During their visits, these missionaries wrote about their Indian contacts and drew maps about the locations of the many tribes of the region. These accounts and maps have proved invaluable to present day historians interested in the history and migration patterns of the Plains Indians.

In the lengthy time period between the Onate expedition and 1719, the Spanish indifference to the Pawnee and Quivira caused the Pawnee to completely forget about their affiliation with the Spanish Crown. Nevertheless, throughout this period the Pawnee made themselves known to the citizens of New Mexico through horse pilfering sorties that proved very successful in supplying horses for the tribes of the Great Plains.

Tension mounted in the fall of 1719 when the governor of New Mexico, Don Antonio Valverde, on a military move to the north against the Comanche, was informed that French traders, trappers, and missionaries were mingling with the Pawnee on the Rio de Jesus Maria. This launched many fears among the Spaniards that the French were taking over the supposedly rich area of Quivira claimed by Spain.

In June of 1720, Valverde organized an expedition at Santa Fe much in the pattern of the expeditions of Coronado and Onate. At the head of the expedition, he placed General Don Pedro de Villasur. Under Villasur was Captain Felipe Tamariz who was in direct charge of the fifty mounted soldiers in the troop and some sixty Pueblo Indian warriors. Tamariz was a conquistador cut from the same mold as Captain Saldivar of the Onate expedition. A strict disciplinarian who lived by the military book, he possessed a slightly cruel streak in his personality and was highly respected by his men and deeply feared by the Indians.

On June 14, 1720, Villasur's expedition began its march north and after traveling to near present-day Scott City, Kansas, about twelve Apache braves were recruited as guides. Since the Apache were enemies of the powerful and large Pawnee tribes, they were eager to assist the Spaniard in a move against them. The presence of the Apache, however, would prove to be out of favor with the Pawnee.

Also traveling with the Spanish army was a Pawnee slave called Francisco Sistaca by the Spaniards. Sistaca had been captured in a Pawnee horse stealing raid into New Mexico and he was brought along to act as an interpreter. Sistaca did not trust the Spaniards nor the Apache so he stayed close to a Friar Martinez who he recognized as a man of God and one who could be trusted.

In late July, the expedition crossed the Republican River. Here the force paused for several days to rest, acquire provisions and heal the feet and aching muscles of both the horses and foot soldiers. In this pause, they did not make contact with any of the Republican Pawnee tribe. Once on the trail again, the expedition moved northeasterly until they reached the Rio de Jesus Maria. Here the caravan crossed and moved easterly along the river until they reached the Loup River which they also crossed. In all the time along the Platte and the Loup rivers, the Spaniards were not in contact with any Indians, but once in the area east of the Loup there were many sightings. On one of these occasions, ten Indians seemed very curious and rode in very close to inspect the caravan. Immediately, Villasur called for Sistaca saying: "Ride forward and try to make conversation with those people."

Riding to within shouting range of the braves, Sistaca spoke out: "I am Sistaca and I am Pawnee. Our leader would like to meet with you to give you a message for your chief." The Indians looked greatly surprised by the red-white man speaking their language and the presence of Apache Indians. Totally confused, they chose to ride off into the distant hills.

The behavior of the Indians disturbed both Villasur and Sistaca. "I know that they understood me because half of them were Pawnee. The others were Oto," said Sistaca. "This is very unusual because I do not remember those tribes ever riding together."

As the caravan continued eastward, they were again scouted closely by Indians on horseback. When these braves were approached again by Sistaca, they withdrew just as the others. The unfriendly attitude of these natives deeply worried Villasur for he had never heard that the Pawnee had ever acted in this manner in their dealings with the Spaniards in the past.

When the Spaniards began to see very large numbers of Indians as they continued to move to the east, Villasur became very troubled. As a result, he ordered his troops to turn around, cross the Loup River, and set up camp in a large open grassy area between the Loup and Platte Rivers.

*   *   *

At the time of the Villasur probe, a large Pawnee earth lodge village near present-day Linwood, Nebraska was the site of a visit by seven Frenchmen and a very large number of Oto braves. The French, who had traveled to this place from Canada, were led by Jean Baptiste Barrios and Francois Mayeux. Barrios, a large hulk of a man dressed in the buckskins of the frontier while Mayeux preferred to dress in the cloth of civilization complete with tri-cornered hat.

This was the first trip of the group to the Pawnee, but they were well-established among the Oto whose main village existed along the Platte several miles from its junction with the Missouri River. When Barrios and Mayeux received word from the Oto and Pawnee scouts that a caravan of white men was in the area, Barrios first called for a meeting with his friend Buratta, war-chief of the Oto contingent.

"The caravan that has been sighted several times by your braves is probably made up of the evil Spaniards," said Barrios to the Oto chief. "It is their goal to place all Indians into slavery and steal their valuables as they did in their sack of Mexico. Their main goal is to become the most powerful nation on earth by stealing from others, including the Pawnee and the Oto."

The words of Barrios angered Buratta and he immediately made plans to visit the Grand Pawnee chief, Gadok, in whose village he and his braves were guests. Reaching the earth lodge of the Pawnee chief, Buratta rapped on one of the supports of the entrance to the shelter. In a few minutes, he was sitting in the warmth of the lodge facing Gadok.

"Barrios has warned me of the nature of the white men we have sighted in the area these last few days," stated Buratta. "They are not friends of the Indian."

"Word has been passed down through the years that the Spaniards have visited the Pawnee in the past and caused us no trouble," answered Gadok.

"Barrios told me that their goal is to steal our valuables to increase the power of their king and that they have already taken all the wealth out of Mexico," added Buratta. Buratta's words disturbed Gadok and he fell into a deep meditation. After several minutes, he continued conversation with the Oto chief.

"Even though the Spaniards have been friendly in the past, I can not understand why Apache Indians are here with them. They may be slaves, but most likely they are allies who would enjoy defeating us. We indeed must take steps to protect our people against this threat."

The more that Gadok thought about the presence of the Spaniards in the area, the more fearful he became. Finally, he asked Buratta to set up a meeting with Barrios and Mayeux the next day because he felt that the existing situation was dangerous to all the people of the Platte. Realizing that Gadok was serious about the urgency of the situation, Buratta hurried to the camp of the French traders to summon them for the meeting proposed for the next day.

Before the sun was high in the sky the next day, Buratta and four Frenchmen, including Barrios and Mayeux, faced Gadok at the center of the earthlodge of the powerful Grand chief.

"I have called all of you here because I feel that as allies we should agree on what to do about the menace of the

Spanish and Apache caravan now camped west of here across the Loup. I am open to any advice that you can give me," said the Pawnee chief as he sat on a comfortable buffalo robe at the end of his large fireplace.

Barrios then stood saying: "We Frenchmen understand the Spaniards much better that the Pawnee or the Oto. For the good of all of us, I think we should attack to drive them away rather than to wait for them to pick the time and the place to attack us."

From a seated position, Buratta issued his opinion: "I agree with my French friend. The past deed of the white men from the southwest show that they cannot be trusted. If they kill and steal from the Indians of Mexico, they will do the same here. I suggest to the great Pawnee chief that we drive them from this land."

When all had spoken, Gadok rose to his feet saying: "Very well, it is agreed that we are in a state of emergency and that we must make plans for war immediately. Before the sun rises in the morning, we must move on the Spaniards and their Apache friends."

Dawn of the next day found the French party of traders and several hundred Pawnee and Oto warriors fording the Platte River from south to north led by Buratta and Gadok. Once the crossing was finished, the massive strike-force continued their march west along the Platte. Shortly after dark, the well-armed party reached the junction with the Loup and here they set up camp for the night, taking care not to light fires or make loud noises.

It was the battle plan to cross the Loup River in the dark and attack the Spanish caravan at daybreak. The composite battle group slept well that night because of their long march the day before. The French traders were the first to rise from their beds early the next day and while stumbling around in the dark, they aroused their Indian allies. Immediately, the French began preparing their muskets for firing and the Oto and Pawnee readied their lances, war clubs, bows and arrows.

Still in the dark, the Indian chiefs ordered their braves into the waters of the Loup and the French interspersed themselves among the braves to lend support. In wading across the river bed, the party found the going rough and many stumbled and fell in the process. Finally, the huge party of wet warriors reached the west bank and there they halted again preparing their weapons for the assault.

As the first rays of sunshine broke in the east, the leaders of the force gazed across the grassy valley to the west. In the distance, they viewed the camp of the Spaniards where no one could be seen stirring. From a military standpoint, things could not have been better for the joined forces.

With one gesture of his muscular arm, Gadok sent the battle group swarming through the grass toward the encampment. As the warriors reached the edge of the camp, some of them slammed their war clubs into the heads of some of the Apache sleeping on the ground.

Within a minute, the death screams and war yelps woke the Spanish soldiers in their tents. They had no time to don their armor. Most just took hold of the first weapon available and tried to stop the onslaught only to be cut down by a volley of arrows or overrun by the large number of Oto or Pawnee. As General Villasur stepped to the opening of his tent, he was met with a heavy lance to his heart and was dead in a moment. Even Friar Martinez who stood waving his arms to try to stop the massacre was soon put away with a crushing tomahawk blow to the head. Both the Spanish soldiers and their Indian allies tried to fight bravely, but the surprise and huge force of savage Indians made quick work of this scattered, unorganized army from New Mexico. Even the Pawnee guide, Sistaca, was killed by the lead ball from a French musket as he tried to call to his Pawnee brothers.

At the height of the fracas, Captain Tamariz tried to get some of his calvary mounted by freeing up seven or eight horses tied at the side of the camp. As the captain drove the horses through a horde of Pawnee braves toward some of his men, seven of the soldiers were able to climb on the steeds and escape slaughter along with Tamariz. Several of the soldiers were wounded and one had been scalped before they could make their flight from the battle scene.

The Villasur massacre was the worst defeat suffered by white men at the hands of Indians in Nebraska. It spelled the end of the influence of the Spanish Crown in the area and it wrote a bitter finale to the series of expensive Spanish expeditions seeking the mines of Quivira, which ironically never existed.

ABOUT THE AUTHOR

Dr. Barak was a World War II navy officer serving in the Pacific Theater. He received a Ph.D. in biochemistry at Missouri University. As a professor, he has taught biochemistry and internal medicine and conducted liver research at the University of Nebraska and Omaha VA Medical Centers for 40 years.

Printed in the United States
66980LVS00004BB/18

9 780595 006205